Kingdom
Parenting

Kingdom Parenting

MYLES MUNROE

AND

DAVID BURROWS

RB BOOKS

Study Guide - Compiled by Jan Sherman

DESTINY IMAGE® PUBLISHERS, INC.
P. O. Box 310, Shippensburg, PA 17257-0310

Published in arrangement with the Original Publisher
DESTINY IMAGE PUBLISHER, INC. USA.

Published in Nigeria

RELIGIOUS BROADCASTING
10, Owoseni Street, Off Mission Road,
Benin City, Edo State.
www.rbbooksng.com, Email: info@rbbooksng.com.
Tel: 08037180294.

SALES OFFICES

17, Bale Street,
Ajegunle, Apapa,
Lagos State.
07067534190

Shop 11 F Line
Ariaria Market,
Aba, Abia State.
07051851731

ISBN 10: 0-7684-2418-6

ISBN 13: 978-0-7684-2418-8

CONTENTS

Part I   **Foundations—Myles Munroe**
Chapter 1   Three Foundational Goals of Parenting 9
Chapter 2   Train Up a Child 21
Chapter 3   Principles of Training Children 33
Chapter 4   Spare Not the Rod. 45
Chapter 5   In Wisdom, Stature, and Favor. 57

Part II   **Building Relationships—David Burrows**
Chapter 6   A Better Tomorrow 69
Chapter 7   The Original Plan 73
Chapter 8   Understanding Teens 79
Chapter 9   Understanding Parents 89
Chapter 10   A Changing World, a Changing Family. 95

Part III   **Connecting Principles—David Burrows**
Chapter 11   Relating to Teens. 109
Chapter 12   Relating to Parents 117
Chapter 13   Practical Wisdom Tips for Parents. 125
Chapter 14   The Word on Parents and Teens 135
Chapter 15   Stories of Hope 141

Part IV   **Study Guide**
             Study Guide Overview. 151
Section 1   Study Questions. 153
Section 2   Part I—Parent Scrapbook. 177
Section 2   Part II—Teen Scrapbook 191
             Journaling and Notes 193

PART I

Foundations

BY MYLES MUNROE

Chapter 1

THREE FOUNDATIONAL GOALS OF PARENTING

By Myles Munroe

*A*s with everything else in life, effective parenting begins with God. Who is better to turn to for the foundational principles of parenting than the Author of life and the Founder of marriage and the family? From the dawn of the human race, God's design has been for us to raise up offspring to populate this planet. Producing and parenting children are a big part of the original mandate humanity received from our Creator:

> Then God said, "Let us make man in our image, in our likeness;..." So God created man in his own image, in the image of God He created him; male and female He created them. God blessed them and said to them, "Be fruitful and increase in number; fill the earth and subdue it. Rule over the fish of the sea and the birds of the air and over every living creature that moves on the ground" (Genesis 1:26-28 NIV).

God's first recorded statement to man established the principle of parenting: "*Be fruitful and increase in number.*" Man was

Key Note:

_____

_____

_____

_____

commanded to reproduce after his own kind and God created "man," both male and female, to make human increase possible through sexual union in the context of marriage. In other words, God created Adam and Eve and then told them to have children. And just as God created Adam and Eve in His own image, their children would in turn bear the image of their parents.

Genesis 5 verifies that Adam and Eve fulfilled this mandate faithfully, as did the generations that succeeded them:

> *This is the written account of Adam's line. When God created man, He made him in the likeness of God. He created them male and female and blessed them. And when they were created, he called them "man." When Adam had lived 130 years, He had a son in his own likeness, in his own image; and he named him Seth* (Genesis 5:1-3 NIV).

God created man (male and female) in His own image and likeness. Notice that the general term "man" includes both male and female; men and women together make up the race that is known as "man" or "mankind." And together they in turn produced children in their image and likeness. The rest of the chapter lists each generation of Adam's descendents up to the days of Noah and his sons. In each case, whether referring to God and man or to parents and their children, the words "image" and "likeness" deal with more than just external appearance; they relate also to internal qualities.

Goal #1: To Reproduce the Nature of the Parent in the Child

From God's original mandate to man to be fruitful, to multiply, and to fill the earth, we can identify three basic goals of parenting. The first goal of parenting is to reproduce the *nature* of the parent in the child. This is part of the meaning behind the word "image." In creation God is Father and mankind are His offspring. By creating us in His image, God intended for us to have and to reflect His nature. In the same way, the first goal human parents should have is to see their nature reproduced in the lives of their children.

Goal #2: To Reproduce the Character of the Parent in the Child

The second goal of parenting is to reproduce the *character* of the parent in the child. This is the other part of "image." The full meaning of the word "image" refers to the true nature and character of a thing. So when God said, "Let us make man in our image, our likeness," He meant, "Let us create man in such a way as to reflect our nature and character." In other words, we were created to be like God: to think like God and to display His distinguishing characteristics—"like Father, like son."

Likewise, human parents want their children to be like them; to share the same values, carry the same demeanor, and display the same characteristics. We have succeeded as parents if people who know us can walk up to our children and say, "You remind me of your daddy," or "You're just like your mama."

Goal #3: To Reproduce the Behavior of the Parent in the Child

Parenting should have the goal of reproducing the *behavior* of the parent in the child. When God created mankind, His goal was to bring about children who were like Himself in every way: children who looked like Him, thought like Him, displayed His characteristics and qualities, and acted like Him. Human parents should pursue the same goal with their children. Ideally,

Key Note:

_____

_____

_____

_____

children should view God and the world and respond to life in the same way their parents do.

Have No Fear

If we want to find the perfect parenting model, we need look no further than the relationship between God the Father and God the Son. Jesus was just like His Father because they were of the same essence. In every way Jesus was the prefect representation of His Father. He even told His disciples plainly, "...*Anyone who has seen me has seen the Father...*" (John 14:9 NIV). Time and again Jesus made it clear that He did nothing on His own but only what He saw His Father doing. (See John 5:19.)

Speaking of Jesus, Paul said in Colossians 1:15, "*He is the image of the invisible God, the firstborn over all creation.*" In other words, Jesus was the perfect reflection of His Father in every way.

Here's an example. One of Jesus' most common phrases to His followers was, "Fear not," or, "Be not afraid," or some other variation of this message. God the Father, as Creator and Lord of all things, fears nothing because He is greater than everything. As a faithful and loyal Son of His father, therefore, Jesus had no fear.

This is one reason why Jesus' life on earth, short as it was, was so powerful and effective. Unlike us, Jesus was never driven or overcome by fear; He was driven only by His Father's will. But He constantly had to comfort and reassure His disciples against being afraid. These were men and women who were supposed to be just like Him, created in the image of God. Patiently and in love He rebuked them for not acting like "Daddy." In fact, one reason Jesus came to earth was to parent us or "re-parent" us, so to speak, by teaching us how to think and act like our heavenly Father.

Paul followed the same tack with Timothy, his son in the faith, when he wrote, "*For God has not given us a spirit of fear, but of power and of love and of a sound mind*" (2 Tim. 1:7 NKJV). God is not a God of fear and, as His children, we should not be children of fear. Likewise, we should raise our children to be free of fear, because our goal as parents is to reproduce children who will be like their parents and, ultimately, like God, the original Parent and Father. Love is the antidote to fear.

John wrote:

> ...God is love. Whoever lives in love lives in God, and God in him. Love is made complete among us so that we will have confidence on the day of judgment, because in this world we are like Him. There is no fear in love. But perfect love drives out fear, because fear has to do with punishment. The one who fears is not made perfect in love (1 John 4:16-18 NIV).

God wants His children to bear His likeness. When we were born again and received the Spirit of God, we received a spirit not of fear but of power, of love, and of a sound mind. This means that the same power that belongs to God belongs to us because we are His children. The same love that characterizes Him, characterizes (or should characterize) us. Our Father's mind should be our mind, as well. In other words, we should be fear-free, power-filled, loving, level-headed people because all these qualities characterize our Father, and we have the same "stuff" He has.

What difference would it make in your life if you could live without fear? What difference would it make in your children's lives if they could do the same?

Key Note:

_____

_____

_____

_____

Be Imitators of God

Sadly, however, most of our children these days live lives that are filled with fear. Why? For one thing, the world can be a fearful place. But the main reason our children live in fear is because we, their parents, live in fear. We have never learned to cast out fear by trusting completely in the perfect love of God—so our children never learn how to do it either. We cannot pass on to our children what we do not possess ourselves.

This is why we cannot live one way and tell our children to live another. Children are great natural learners and they learn best through observation and imitation. If our words say one thing and our actions another, our children will pick up on our actions and ignore our words. For this reason we must be very careful to live the way we want our children to live.

The old adage, "Do as I say, not as I do" is a recipe for parental failure. Our children learn much more from our example than they do from our words, especially if our example and our words do not agree. Words and examples that reinforce each other, on the other hand, work to great effect in reproducing our nature, character, and behavior in our children.

Parenting is powerful because it shapes the minds, attitudes, and actions of our children for either good or bad. An ancient proverb says: "*Even a child is known by his actions, by whether his conduct is pure and right*" (Prov. 20:11 NIV). Children learn their behavior by watching and imitating the people they see the most, usually parents, especially during the child's formative years.

So how can we set the right kind of example for our children? By referring, as always, to the Bible, the instruction manual provided by God, the original Parent. Paul, who knew something about spiritual parenting, wrote: "*Be imitators of God, therefore, as dearly loved children and live a life of love, just as Christ loved us and gave himself up for us as a fragrant offering and sacrifice to God*" (Eph. 5:1-2 NIV).

How do we imitate God? By living a life of love. Remember, love is the antidote to fear. And how do we know how to model love? By looking to Christ as our example. Jesus modeled the nature, character, and behavior of His Father, and if we imitate Him in word and deed, we will provide our children with a reliable model on which to pattern their own lives.

Parenting Must Be Intentional

No one parents effectively by accident. Effective parenting must be intentional; it must be planned, focused, and have an expected end in mind. Good parents don't leave the job to chance; they do everything they can to prepare themselves and to know what they are doing.

Even for conscientious parents, however, there are a couple of major challenges to deal with in raising children well. The first of these is the simple truth that parents can only parent the way they themselves were parented. In other words, no matter how conscientious you are in your desire to parent your children well, if your own parents did a poor job—if they failed to model the love and character and behavior of God before you—you likely will have a difficult time overcoming the effects of their example. Try as hard as you will, there will be times when things get tough as a parent and you will find it very easy to slide into the pattern established by your own parents, because that is what is most familiar—and most comfortable. Learning solid biblical

Key Note:

_____

_____

_____

_____

principles of parenting is the key to breaking those negative patterns, but it will require serious and continuing effort.

The second challenge we all must deal with as parents is the reality of sinful human nature both in ourselves and in our children. Genesis 5 says that Adam produced children and descendants in his own likeness and image. He did a good job; like Adam, we all are "perfect sinners." Adam was so "effective" in his parenting that when he fell, his descendants fell. We inherited his sin nature. The Bible says that because of Adam's disobedience, disobedience entered into the hearts of every human being.

Because all human beings are sinners, none of us had perfect parents and none of us will be perfect parents. All we can do is learn the biblical principles, commit our way as parents unto the Lord, and trust Him to work powerfully in our children's lives beyond what we can do on our own.

Sin essentially is rebellion, and it is deeply rooted in all our hearts. Anyone who is a parent knows that rebellion is in the hearts of their children from birth. You don't have to teach your child to lie; lying is "built in." You don't have to teach your child to be jealous of your affection toward another child or to be greedy for another child's toy; your child comes by these traits "naturally." This is why the Bible says, *"Foolishness is bound up in the heart of a child; The rod of correction will drive it far from him"* (Prov. 22:15 NKJV). Where did this foolishness come from? By direct lineal descent from Adam, the first human father. And the "rod of correction" refers to disciplined, deliberate, conscientious, purposeful, and intentional parenting.

Whether negative or positive, parenting is a powerful and inescapable influence. Everybody is parented by somebody. We each reflect in our lives and our attitudes the nature, character, and behavior of those who have influenced us the most. We tend to become like the person who parents us and he or she may or may not be our biological parent. This is true also for our children. You can be a father or a mother and still not be a parent, because a "parent" is the one who has the most formative influence in a child's life.

Consider the implications of this: Who parents your children? Who has the greatest daily or ongoing influence over their growth and development? A schoolteacher? A daycare worker? A babysitter? Television programmers? Either you parent your children or someone else will, because children are not equipped to raise themselves. They will find guidance somewhere, and unless you provide it, you may not like the results.

My oldest brother and his wife told me a story once about their daughter and her daycare center. The two of them are elders in their church. They love the Lord and are raising their children to love and serve Him, as well. One day when their daughter was two or three, she dropped something or hit her hand and uttered a four-letter curse word. Her parents were shocked. They said, "What did you say?" So she repeated it, because she thought they really wanted to hear it again. This man and woman of God, who are church elders and are full of God's Word, had just heard their precious daughter speak a word she had never heard at home!

As a result, my sister-in-law called the daycare center and spoke to the director: "What kind of language do you allow the children to speak? Our daughter is saying a word we don't appreciate and have never taught her. Can you explain this to us?"

The director "explained" that they were planning to move their daughter from upstairs to downstairs because the upstairs

Key Note:

_____

_____

_____

_____

children upstairs talked that way. What kind of an answer is that? My brother and sister-in-law both found it necessary to work and were paying good money to a daycare center that was teaching their daughter things that were opposite to what she was being taught at home!

Don't misunderstand me; my point here is not to evaluate the benefits or deficits of daycare. My point is this: *who's parenting your children?* Conscientious parents must be on constant guard to protect their children from negative formative influences. Effective parenting *must* be intentional!

Righteous and Godly Offspring

The three primary goals of parenting are to reproduce in children the nature, character, and behavior of their parents. According to the standards established by the Creator in the beginning, parenthood takes place properly only within the context of marriage. So marriage is the vehicle God established through which children are to be brought into the world. By design, all children are supposed to have two parents: a mother and a father who are married to each other. Believing parents have the responsibility to raise righteous and godly children. In fact, the Bible even says that this is one of God's primary purposes for marriage:

> *Have we not all one Father? Did not one God create us? Why do we profane the covenant of our fathers by breaking faith with one another?* (Malachi 2:10 NIV).

This verse stresses two things: first, that God is our Father and second, that marriage is the context through which God wants to father us. The "covenant" here refers not only to the spiritual covenant God made with the nation of Israel, but also to the covenant of marriage, which is a visual symbol of the spiritual covenant. That marriage in view here is made clear several verses later:

...the Lord is acting as the witness between you and the wife of your youth, because you have broken faith with her, though she is your partner, the wife of your marriage covenant. Has not the Lord made them one? In flesh and spirit they are his. And why one? Because he was seeking godly offspring. So guard yourself in your spirit, and do not break faith with the wife of your youth (Malachi 2:14-15 NIV).

The nation of Israel was in deep trouble because they had abandoned their covenant with God and began to serve foreign gods. Also, the Lord no longer paid attention to their offerings, in large part because they were breaking the marriage covenant through divorce, thereby disrupting God's plan and desire to raise up "godly offspring." God not only wants to father us; He also wants to father godly offspring *through* us. What an awesome responsibility—and *privilege!*

Ultimately, marriage is not for us as much as it is for God. Marriage, as Paul tells us in Ephesians 5:31-32, is a picture of the relationship between Christ and the Church. Two people become one flesh. And Malachi says that God made them one because He was seeking godly offspring. In effect, God is saying that the whole point of marriage is so He can have some people through whom He can parent kids.

So the primary purpose of parenting is to produce righteous and godly children for God. The word "righteous" means "right positioning" or "to be in right relationship." In other words, the

Key Note:

_____

_____

_____

_____

purpose of parenting is to raise up children who are in right relationship with God—children who are in line with God's will and who desire to please Him—children who reflect His nature.

This involves nurturing and training a child's conscience to be tuned toward God. A conscience bent toward pleasing God will help children avoid sinful or destructive behavior, not out of duty but out of love. They will desire to please God because they love Him. The proof of good parenting is seen in how our children behave in our absence. If they do the right thing for their conscience's sake, even when we are not around, we have succeeded as parents. We have raised righteous children.

The word "godly" means "god-like." Godly children are children who reflect not only God's nature but also His character and His behavior. Here is where the challenge really comes in for parents. We cannot hope to raise godly children unless we are firmly committed to living as godly parents. This means we must allow God to shape and mold and direct our wills and our hearts—we must allow God to Father us—so that we become faithful, loving children who do His will out of love and thereby model godly character and behavior for our children. In this way God can fulfill His plan and desire of fathering godly offspring through us.

Biblical wisdom says, "*Train a child in the way he should go, and when he is old he will not turn from it*" (Prov. 22:6 NIV). There is nothing more worthwhile or of greater importance in this world than for parents to commit themselves to living godly lives and raising righteous and godly children who love the Lord their God with all their heart, soul, mind, and strength. This is God's design. This is His plan. And this is the purpose of parenting.

Chapter 2

TRAIN UP A CHILD

BY MYLES MUNROE

If the purpose of parenting is to raise righteous and godly children, the question naturally arises: how do we accomplish this? *How* do we raise children who are in right standing with God, who love Him with all their heart, and who live godly lives? The answer is very simple: *training.* As parents, we must train our children deliberately and purposefully, and this requires planning. This is why I said in the last chapter that parenting must be intentional. Training does not happen by default. Godly children do not turn out by accident; they are the product of the efforts of committed, godly parents.

There is a lot of information on parenting in the world today, probably more than ever before. Some of it is sound, but much of it is not, because it is based on philosophies and world views that are the products of men's minds rather than the mind of God. For wise counsel on raising godly children it is best to refer to the original source material: God's Word, as recorded in the Bible. With this in mind, I will focus in this chapter on three

Key Note:

_____

_____

_____

_____

Scriptures that provide fundamental guidelines for training children. In the next chapter I will deal more specifically with principles of training and discipline.

Know the Way—Show the Way

The Book of Proverbs is an excellent resource for conscientious parents because much of it was written from the perspective of a father giving wise counsel to his son. Perhaps the most fundamental child-training principle of all is the Scripture I cited at the close of the last chapter: "*Train a child in the way he should go, and when he is old he will not turn from it*" (Prov. 22:6 NIV). We could call this the "Parents' Mandate." Our basic job as parents is to teach our children to think right, talk right, and live right—to show them the right way to live. Sounds easy enough, don't you think? But right away we face a couple of big challenges.

First of all, in order to show the way to our children we must know the way ourselves. If we don't know the way, how can we show the way? How can we train our children to live right if we don't know how to live right? How can we teach them to pray if we don't know how to pray? How can we teach them God's Word if we don't know God's Word? How will our children learn to trust God in all things if we do not model that trust for them in our own lives? Our children can go only where we, their parents, take them.

So our first job as parents is to study and know for ourselves the way that our children should go so that we can show them the way. And what is the way? It is the way of righteousness and godliness. That's a tough assignment for parents (or anyone else)! And this is where we find our second big challenge. Why? Because learning the way of righteousness and godliness is a lifelong process for us as well as for our children. So, even as we are learning the way, we must model it and teach it so our children will learn to follow our example.

This is why it is so important for young couples to be qualified for parenthood before they get married. There is a lot more to qualifying for parenthood than possessing the biological and physiological ability to conceive and bear children. Remember, the main purpose for marriage is to produce godly offspring for God. No matter how old you are, if you do not know and are not learning the way of righteous and godly living, you are not ready for either marriage or for parenthood.

Parents who know the way show the way so that their children will grow into fruitful, productive, fulfilled adults who reflect in their lives the likeness of Christ—His nature, character, and behavior. There is no greater gift and no more powerful legacy parents can pass on to their children than to train them in the way of the Lord and to teach them to love Him with all their hearts. Such a legacy helps our children discover that meaning and purpose in life are found in living consciously and deliberately as citizens of the Kingdom of Heaven.

It is this legacy that brings us to the second part of Proverbs 22:6: if we train our children in the way they should go, when they are old they *will not turn from it.* God is saying to parents, "Don't worry about your children. If you did your job properly, you have them for life. They will love Me and live for Me forever."

I have ten siblings. My parents raised 11 children, and all of us know Jesus. Mom and dad never had much money. Although they were not able to provide for us with much in the way of material things or worldly wealth, they always put food on the

Key Note:

_____

_____

_____

_____

table and clothes on our backs. We were never hungry or cold. Even more importantly, they gave us in abundance what money could never buy: love. Every one of us 11 kids felt equally loved. Mom and dad taught us to love God. And they taught us how to live.

In an environment such as that, what difference did it make if we were "poor" in material things? We were rich in the things that really matter: love of God, love of family, love of life, and the knowledge and the confidence to live life abundantly. What more could we have needed?

One of the reasons my parents succeeded with their children is because they understood that parenting is intentional and must begin immediately upon the birth of each child. Waiting until children are teenagers to get serious about training them is too late. It is never too early to begin training a child. Even infants learn quickly and benefit significantly from a deliberate parental plan of training and instruction.

Repeated studies have made it clear that children learn everything they need to learn in their first seven years of life. After age seven, children learn only what they want to learn. In other words, if you do not train your children in the way they should go by the time they are seven—if you do not nurture in them your nature, character, and behavior by then—you probably never will. But if you do show them the way by age seven, it is highly likely they will follow that road all their lives. They may "test the waters" or "sow their wild oats" for a time, as young people often do, but most of the time they eventually return to the values, beliefs, and training they received as children. That is the promise of the proverb which says to train a child in the way he should go, and when he is *old* he will not turn from it.

Don't forget that as humans we are spiritual beings housed in physical bodies. Unlike our physical bodies, our spirits are ageless. When we begin training our children, that training goes right into their ageless spirit where it takes root and begins to grow. Normally the growth of a child's spirit outstrips his or her physical growth. So when a properly trained child tends to be led astray by the fleshly urges and desires of a still-maturing body, the child's spirit can assert its supremacy and draw that child back into walking the "straight and narrow" path of his or her early training. The training of the child's formative years prevails so that the child, when old, will not turn from it.

Know the way and show the way. That is the surest way to bring up godly offspring.

Children Cannot Raise Themselves

Modeling the right way to live for our children is critical to their health, welfare, and success. This should be self-evident, yet I am continually amazed at how many parents today essentially leave their children to fend for themselves. And then they wonder why their kids rebel, suffer from depression, become suicidal, have problems in school, and get into trouble with the law.

Economic realities in many households make it necessary for both parents to work, and job demands take their toll on the amount of time parents are able to spend with their children. Many other factors come into play as well that distract parents from giving proper attention to their parental responsibilities. Quite often, older siblings, while still children themselves, are left in charge of their younger brothers and sisters. This is both tragic and wrong because children are unable to raise themselves and should never be expected to.

Key Note:

_____

_____

_____

_____

Once again, the Book of Proverbs provides wise counsel: "*The rod of correction imparts wisdom, but a child left to himself disgraces his mother*" (Prov. 29:15 NIV). God never intended children to raise themselves. Humans are not designed for self-raising. That's what parents are for: to love, nurture, care for, and train children to become mature, happy, successful, productive, and well-adjusted adults. Yet, how often do we see this scenario: parents go off to work on the second shift (or to party) and leave a list for their kids, perhaps as young as six: "Supper's in the 'fridge'; heat it up; wash the dishes, wash the clothes, do your homework, close the windows, leave the porch light on, and go to bed?" This is too much to put on a child.

Someone might ask, "Well, what about teaching children responsibility?" Teaching children age-appropriate responsibility is one thing; placing on them burdens they were never meant to carry is another. Teaching a six-year-old to put his toys away and place his dirty clothes in the laundry hamper is appropriate responsibility; putting him in charge of preparing supper for his four-year-old sister is not. Age-appropriate responsibility means training children and assigning tasks to them according to their *ability* to *respond* (which is what the word "responsibility" means).

Placing a six-year-old in charge of his younger siblings is not responsible—it's abuse. Giving children responsibilities that are inappropriate for their age and development delegates to them something they are not built to carry. The effects may not be visible immediately but over the long term, psychological damage will occur. They will grow up being resentful of their brothers and sisters and bitter toward their parents for robbing them of their childhood.

God designed children for play. That's how they learn, how they become creative, how they grow. Children learn to socialize and relate to other people properly through play, not through work.

Children are not merely pint-sized adults, and it is wrong to treat them as such. They need patient guidance, careful instruction, consistent discipline, and clearly defined boundaries. All of these things are vital for a child's sense of safety and security. Children must feel safe and secure if they are to grow up free of fear, anxiety, and psychological problems. However, many children today feel like little more than slaves or indentured servants in their own homes. Their parents expect too much of them and make too many demands on them. Children should not be expected to serve their parents, but parents for their children.

Our responsibility as parents is not to train up good workers to take care of us but to raise righteous offspring. Children should be given increased responsibilities as they grow older, according to their ability to understand and their demonstrated capability to bear those responsibilities. They must be both physically and emotionally mature enough to handle the tasks required of them.

One Proverb I quoted above says that "*a child left to himself disgraces his mother.*" This is another way of saying that the behavior of children reflects on their parents. If a child is headed in the wrong direction, most of the time it is due to the parents' failure to train the child in the way he or she should go. I say, "most of the time," because children, like adults, possess free wills, and sometimes children who have been raised right and trained right by their parents still choose to go in the wrong direction.

Key Note:

_____

_____

_____

_____

For the most part, however, the behavior of children is a very revealing indicator of the kind and quality of parenting they have received. Parents who place no boundaries on their children raise children who run wild. Parents who cheat and are dishonest raise children who have no respect for authority. Parents who constantly belittle and demean their children program their children for failure.

On the other hand, parents who create an environment of affirming love, fair and consistent discipline, and challenging but realistic expectations produce children who are confident, secure, high achievers, and mentally, socially, and emotionally well-adjusted individuals. Parents who love the Lord supremely and model that love continually raise children who have the same affections.

Children cannot raise themselves, and God never meant for them to. They look to us, their parents, to train them and raise them for spiritual strength in God and for success in life.

Provoke Not Your Children to Wrath

The third fundamental Scripture on child rearing I want to examine in this chapter comes from apostle Paul in the New Testament: "*And, ye fathers, provoke not your children to wrath: but bring them up in the nurture and admonition of the Lord*" (Eph. 6:4). To "provoke" means to "exasperate," as another translation of this verse indicates: "*Fathers, do not exasperate your children; instead, bring them up in the training and instruction of the Lord*" (Eph. 6:4 NIV).

This does not mean that as parents we should avoid ever making our children angry. If we are responsible, conscientious parents who are committed to raising our children well, it is inevitable that at times we will say or do something that our children will not like or appreciate. There are times when our actions and decisions on their behalf will make them angry and it may be many years before they understand why we did what we did. When Paul says, "Provoke not" or "Do not exasperate" our children, he is not talking about the everyday realities of parenting, but inconsistencies in our behavior toward our children.

One way we exasperate our children is by demonstrating double standards in front of them. This is the old "Do as I say, not as I do" trap. We tell our kids one thing and then do another. We tell our children to be honest in all their dealings and then we cheat on our taxes. We teach them not to lie and then when someone we don't want to talk to is on the phone, we say to our child, "Tell him I'm not at home." Children become confused and exasperated with parents who have double standards. They don't know how to act or what to do. Double standards destroy a child's sense of safety and security because there is no consistency of behavior. Our children need the reassurance of knowing that what we say or do on one occasion is the same thing we will say or do when a similar occasion arises. They need to know we can be trusted.

Another way we exasperate our children is by making unrealistic threats or failing to follow through with our word. Suppose you are in the habit of saying to your children things like, "If you do that again, I'll break your neck!" Do this often enough and over time one of two things will happen: either your child will believe you and develop an unhealthy fear of you, or your child will not believe you and soon he or she will come to disregard all your threats as meaningless. Either way you are headed for trouble with your child. If you tell your child you are

Key Note:

_____

_____

_____

_____

going to spank him or her when you get home, do it. Follow through. The long-term benefit the child will receive is reassurance that you are consistent and can be trusted; this will far outweigh the short-term pain and unpleasantness of the spanking.

A similar problem occurs when you make a promise to your child and then fail to follow through. Children remember these things and, as they grow older, resentment grows stronger in them. If you promise to take them for ice cream after they clean their rooms, do it. Be consistent. Follow through with what you say so that your children will know that you are true to your word. In this way they will trust you and believe you when you talk to them about the truly important things in life.

Inconsistent discipline is another area where parents often exasperate their children. As parents, we must be careful always to make discipline (in the sense of punishment) commensurate with the offense and ensure that it is administered equitably, fairly, and consistently. Our children deserve to know reliably what to expect.

Another problem to avoid is creating the perception that one child is favored over another. If one child is given preferential treatment, the other children will become resentful toward the parents as well as toward the favored sibling. This is what happened to Joseph in the Old Testament. Joseph's brothers hated him because they knew he was the favorite son of their father, Jacob. Jacob's preferential treatment of Joseph exasperated his other sons. Their hatred became so intense that eventually they sold their brother Joseph into slavery. Then they lied to their father about Joseph's fate. These other sons of Jacob became hard, embittered men whose behavior over the years brought much trouble upon their father, their families, and themselves.

It is important that we make sure to love all our children equally and never show favoritism.

Know the way and show the way. Don't leave your children to fend for themselves. Be consistent in all your words and behavior so as not to exasperate your children or provoke them to wrath and rebellion. These are the fundamental guidelines that will help you succeed as parents in your God-given responsibility and privilege to train your children in the way they should go so that when they are old they will not turn from it.

Key Note:

_____

_____

_____

_____

Chapter 3

Principles of Training Children

By Myles Munroe

The lives and welfare of future generations depend on how effective we are today as parents in training our children. Make no mistake about it: the quality of our parenting today will be reflected not only in the lives, values, and attitudes of our children but also in the lives of their children and their children's children. Our success or failure as parents will have long-term, multigenerational consequences. That is why we must be very careful to get a good handle on training and learn to raise our children properly.

In the last chapter we pointed out that children need training. Children are not born self-sufficient or possessing the knowledge they need to live successfully; they must be trained. We also saw that children cannot raise or train themselves. God gave that responsibility to parents—to us—and He holds us accountable for the way we bring up our children. In addition, training, like all of parenting, must be intentional. It must be deliberate. Training will not take place by accident.

Key Note:

_____

_____

_____

_____

And because of its multigenerational influence, training must be pursued with a clear view to the long term. Our goal as parents is not merely to elicit immediate obedience and obtain instant results but to lay a firm foundation for the future: to train our children in the way they should go so that when they are old they will not turn from it but will walk in that way and pass it on to their own children.

Training benefits both parent and child. Children benefit from training because it prepares them for life. Parents benefit because well-trained, well-raised children return to bless, honor, and respect them. Effective parenting carries a *quid pro quo*: if it is the parents' responsibility not to provoke or exasperate their children, it is the children's responsibility to obey their parents. In the verses immediately preceding his instructions against parents exasperating their children, Paul says:

> *Children, obey your parents in the Lord, for this is right.*
> *"Honor your father and mother"—which is the first command-*
> *ment with a promise—"that it may go well with you and that*
> *you may enjoy long life on the earth"* (Ephesians 6:1-3 NIV).

What benefits accrue to children who honor and obey their parents? The first one is stated directly in the passage above: *long life*. Obedience promotes long life not only because God honors obedience but also because obeying one's parents, with their greater maturity, knowledge, and experience, can help one avoid unnecessary dangers and pitfalls in life.

Second, obedience to one's parents helps develop discipline in one's life. One of the fundamental truths that children must learn is that they cannot have everything they want or do anything they please. Life and personal freedom have limits, and obedience to parental and other authorities helps children learn this lesson. Obedience fosters discipline by teaching children the value of delayed gratification and the necessity of subordinating their own desires at times in favor of the needs and desires of others.

A third benefit of obedience for children is that it helps them develop a submissive spirit. It's extremely difficult to submit to God without first learning how to submit to legitimate human authority. That is why God gave all of us parents. Learning to submit to and obey their earthly parents teaches children how to obey their invisible heavenly Parent. And not only to obey Him but also to *love* Him. Submission, properly expressed, is a freewill act of love. Strange as it may sound, children learn to love God by submitting to their parents.

Finally, children benefit from obedience to their parents because it teaches them respect for authority. One characteristic of well-raised children is that they recognize, respect, submit to, and obey legitimate authority figures in their lives. They understand that authority-and-command structures are vital parts of a secure and stable society, and they are indispensable in promoting and preserving true freedom—freedom within limits.

Control: The Prerequisite for Training

Every schoolteacher knows that he or she cannot teach students unless they can control their classrooms. The same is true with parenting: we cannot train our children until and unless we can first control our children. This may seem self-evident, but it is amazing how many parents essentially ignore this principle in practice. They attempt to teach or train their children without first establishing clear ground rules as to who is in charge, and then they wonder why their children are unresponsive.

Key Note:

_____

_____

_____

_____

This question of control becomes a major issue where blended families are concerned. Stepparents often encounter difficulties in gaining the respect of their stepchildren; and with no respect there can be no control. How many loving stepparents have heard the frustrating and heartbreaking words, "You can't tell me what to do; you're not my mother!" or "I don't have to listen to you; you're not my *real* dad!" Whether their family is a blended family or a traditional family, the parents must find a workable way of exercising consistent, firm but fair control over all the children in the family. Otherwise, there will be a great deal of chaos, confusion, conflict, heartache, and dysfunction and very little effective training.

Single parents face control challenges of their own, but of a different kind. For the most effective results, children, regardless of gender, need the parental guidance of both a mother and a father; this is the way God designed the family. Moms or dads who are raising their children alone face the daunting task of trying to fill both parental roles. The challenge is the same whether it was death or divorce that caused the loss of the other parent. As with a blended family, firm control of the children by a single parent is absolutely essential in order to avoid chaos and to accomplish effective training.

Divorced parents who do not have primary custody of their children face perhaps the biggest challenge of all. It's not easy to train children you only see a few hours at a time or only a couple of weekends every month. And if the two "exes" disagree on the object, means, and specifics of training, this only adds to the problem. Children who operate under one set of rules at home and a completely different set of rules when they are with the other parent, often end up confused, insecure, and with a feeling of being caught in the middle. A common childhood and adolescent response to this kind of stress is rebellion.

A few simple guidelines may be of enormous value in helping parents exercise effective control of their children so training can take place. Please note, however, that *simple* does not necessarily mean *easy*. The guidelines are simple in concept but may not be simple in execution.

First of all, tailor your control and training to the age and development of the child. For example, don't try to reason with a very young child. Young children need clear, firm guidelines to direct their behavior until their reasoning ability matures, usually sometime around junior-high age.

Second, be consistent. Don't give in to the temptation to relax your standards or your expectations. Your children need and deserve the security and stability of always knowing what to expect from you and what you expect from them. They may balk and complain and scream and cry and kick against your rules, but stand firm. The moment you give in, you surrender control to your children and all hope of training them disappears.

Third, be in agreement with your spouse. As much as possible, the two of you should be in complete agreement regarding how you will raise your children. You should agree on what you will allow, what you will not allow, and what the penalties will be for infractions. You should agree never to disagree in front of the children, but maintain a united front. This will go far in dismantling one of the favorite control tactics of children: playing one parent against the other.

Fourth, don't try to be your children's "buddy." You're not their buddy; you're their parent, and that's what they need you to be. They need someone who will affirm and encourage them

Key Note:

_____

_____

_____

_____

when they're right, and correct and redirect them when they're wrong, while loving them consistently throughout.

Training Often Involves Coercion

Training does not come naturally to children. Like everyone else, children have a mind of their own and tend to resist the training that will place restraints on their freedom or activities. That's why training must be intentional, deliberate, and planned on the part of the parents. A healthy dose of patience will help also. Rarely will any training "take" the first time with a child; it will be necessary to repeat the lesson on numerous occasions until the child internalizes it and begins to do it on his own. Even then, occasional reminders or encouragement will be needed.

Sometimes verbal instruction alone will provide insufficient motivation for a child to obey. On those occasions, other, more forceful or coercive methods may be required. The Bible refers to this as the "*rod of correction*" or "*rod of discipline*" (Prov. 22:15). This phrase includes but is not limited to coercive force or corporal punishment. "Rod" may also refer to a standard of measure, a standard of behavior and character to which children are held accountable.

Children are not born holy. They do not come into the world with a heart that is bent toward obedience. They must be taught to obey. They must be taught to honor and respect their parents. They must be taught to love God. While children cannot be forced or coerced into loving God, careful, loving, intentional training and discipline, including judicious application of the "rod of correction," can help form in children a humble and submissive (not broken!) spirit that is open to receiving and responding to the love of God. (The issue of the "rod of correction" and its application will be discussed in greater detail in the next chapter.)

In the midst of today's cultural and social climate that is especially sensitive (and rightfully so) to the issues of physical and sexual abuse of children, any discussion of coercive measures in child training is fraught with many potential hazards. Let me be straightforward and blunt: *any kind of abuse of children, whether physical, mental, verbal, or sexual abuse, is absolutely wrong!* It is a crime against the child and against society, and it is a sin before the God who created children and loves them dearly. Coercive training methods, when necessary, are not for beating a child into submission, but for correcting him or her in love. They are for the purpose of reinforcing the training, not breaking the child's spirit.

Because of the ease with which they may slip over the line into abuse, coercive training measures should be applied carefully, appropriately, and sparingly. *Carefully* means after deliberated thought and never impulsively or in the heat of anger. *Appropriately* means proportional to the offense and not always the measure of first resort. The "rod" of physical coercion is not appropriate in every situation. *Sparingly* means applied rarely, perhaps for specific infractions or as a measure of last resort when other measures have proven ineffective (but never out of anger or frustration, even as a last resort).

Two additional important considerations with regard to coercive training measures relate to the appropriate *location* on the body for applying the rod and the appropriate *instrument* of application. Concerning the location, it is *never* appropriate to

Key Note:

_____

_____

_____

_____

strike a child in the face in any manner whatsoever. Punching, slapping, pinching, or pulling a child's face is always wrong and amounts to abuse. The same holds true for the child's neck, back, chest, stomach, arms, hair, and legs. A child is not a punching bag.

God built into the design of the human body an appropriate spot for the application of corporal discipline: the buttocks with their ample natural padding and sensitive nerve endings. In fact, this is the only suitable place on the body for applying physical persuasion. The Bible says, "*Do not withhold discipline from a child; if you punish him with the rod, he will not die. Punish him with the rod and save his soul from death*" (Prov. 23:13-14 NIV). So don't be afraid to train and to enforce discipline, but when physical measures are called for, use the appropriate location. Apply your discipline to the well-padded spot.

But apply it with what? What instrument of application is appropriate for coercive measures in training? Not your hand; never your hand. Why not? Because children should always associate their parents' hands with love and affection, never with pain and punishment. The very phrase "rod of correction" implies an instrument that is external to the body. It could be a belt, a paddle—anything that will produce a stinging pain to the buttocks yet cause no injury or physical harm to the child. In this way the child will learn to associate the pain and discomfort with their wrong behavior and with the instrument of discipline, not with the hand of the parent who administers it.

The divine instrument of discipline is love, not the rod. The rod communicates love; it is the administration of love. Scripture says, "*He who spares the rod hates his son, but he who loves him is careful to discipline him*" (Prov. 13:24). Corrective coercive discipline is an act of love that is designed to redirect a child's thoughts, attitude, and behavior back onto the right path. It is an essential part of training a child in the way he or she should go so that correct thinking, attitudes, and behavior will become his or her lifestyle.

Discipline Looks to the Future

Discipline is indispensable in the life of children because it helps prepare them for the future. The Bible says, "*Discipline your son, for in that there is hope; do not be a willing party to his death*" (Prov. 19:18). This verse tells us at least two things. First, discipline and hope are linked and, secondly, by implication, lack of discipline is linked to death. Hope refers to future expectation. The lesson seems clear: if we want our children to live long and enjoy a bright future tomorrow, we must discipline them today. Our failure to discipline, on the other hand, could be deadly; it might even destroy their future.

No responsible parent enjoys disciplining his or her children. The old saying, "This is going to hurt me more than it hurts you," carries a lot of truth. Discipline is a painful process for both parent and child. But it must be done in order to ensure the child's future. Today's pain brings tomorrow's gain. We discipline our children today so that they will learn to discipline themselves tomorrow when we are no longer around.

Applying discipline inappropriately can be just as harmful as not applying any discipline at all. With that in mind, here are ten simple principles or guidelines to help ensure that the discipline you apply is appropriate, effective, and is received by your children in the spirit you intended.

Key Note:

_____

_____

_____

_____

1. Be consistent.

Don't keep your kids guessing about what you expect from them or what they can expect from you. Set clear boundaries and guidelines and stick to them.

2. Never discipline in anger.

Discipline plus anger usually results in abuse, not correction. Once that line is crossed, whatever training goal you had is forfeited.

3. Treat all your children equally.

Favoritism (even *perceived* favoritism) fosters bitterness and resentment in the hearts of the children who feel they have been slighted. Discipline should always be age-appropriate, but within that parameter, every child should receive the same treatment.

4. Never allow your children to despise discipline.

If after being disciplined your children run off muttering or cursing or slamming doors or stomping their feet or continuing to act out with other inappropriate behaviors, they obviously have missed the point of the discipline (provided your discipline was appropriate and proportional in the first place). Go to them and reapply the discipline, explaining that they need to understand and respect the reason for it. The proper response from them is not rebellion and defiance but submission.

5. Do not allow your children to rebel.

Rebellion calls for sterner disciplinary measures than before. Help your children understand that obedience is the quickest path to getting what they want. It's a lot less painful, too.

6. Do not allow your children to complain about their discipline.

If appropriate, allow and encourage your children to share their side of the story or to explain their behavior *before* discipline is determined. Once the appropriate course of action is decided, however, all discussion is over. Proceed promptly to the administration of discipline.

7. Do not allow your children to become bitter.

Sometimes you may discipline wrongly because you do not have all the information. No one's perfect. If this happens, go to your child, confess your error, and apologize. Your children know you make mistakes, but it will do them a world of good to know also that you are not afraid to admit it. This will quench any sparks of bitterness that may be simmering in their hearts.

8. Do not allow your children to become slothful.

Undisciplined children become lazy children at home and in life. They become mentally unfocused, lacking drive and a sense of purpose. Prevent sloth in your children by making sure that they are involved in productive activity in the home. Assign them age-appropriate tasks and hold them accountable for those chores. Teach them how to be responsible. They may chafe under it today but they will thank you tomorrow.

9. Never ask or demand your children to do anything you would not do.

Aside from being hypocritical, it places them in an unfair position of having to choose between obeying you or following their conscience.

10. Never ridicule, belittle, scorn, or embarrass your children, especially in public.

This applies especially to older children. Younger children usually are not highly self-conscious and therefore can be corrected in public without feeling humiliated. As children grow

Key Note:

_____

_____

_____

_____

older, however, they begin to develop a sense of pride, which is a good thing. Children need to be able to have appropriate pride in themselves. When correction and discipline are needed while in public, be careful to administer it in such a way as to preserve their pride and dignity. If possible, get away with them privately and deal with the situation. Otherwise, speak to them as unobtrusively as possible. The object is correction, not humiliation. Humiliating an older child in public, especially in front of his or her friends, can be devastating to him or her, and it will easily lead to bitterness, resentment, rebellion, and all sorts of other behavioral and attitudinal problems.

Chapter 4

SPARE NOT THE ROD

BY MYLES MUNROE

*D*iscipline, as we saw in the preceding chapter, is an act of love by parents who are seeking to train their children in the right way to live and think. And although discipline should be an indispensable and ongoing part of training our children, it should *not* be constant. To be effective (as well as fair), discipline should be applied only when necessary.

The Scripture says, "*He who spares his rod hates his son, But he who loves him disciplines him promptly*" (Prov. 13:24 NKJV). The word "promptly" has to do with timeliness. Discipline, therefore, should be administered in a timely manner, implying that there are times when discipline is *not* timely. In other words, discipline is not always necessary.

Unfortunately, some parents seem not to understand this. Have you ever known parents who seemed unable to say anything to their children that wasn't some kind of criticism or correction, even when the children appeared to be doing nothing wrong? Even more to the point, are you ever guilty of this as a

Key Note:

_____

_____

_____

_____

parent? Constant criticism and correction by one's parents produces an insecure child who is uncertain of his or her parents' love, locking the child into a "performance" mentality where he or she constantly tries to earn the love and acceptance that is missing.

Here's some good advice for every parent, and especially those who tend to be overly critical and demanding: *Relax! Lighten up! Have fun with your kids!* Sit down with them and talk about life. Find out how they're doing and get their perspective on things. Every day you spend with your kids you are creating memories, so what kind of memories do you want them to have? How do you want your children to remember you in years to come: as a parent who could laugh and have fun and love and affirm them openly, or as a parent who was never satisfied with them?

I couldn't begin to count the number of troubled kids who have come to me about their parents, saying, "I can never do nothing right for her," or "Dad doesn't appreciate me. No matter what I try to do, it's always wrong." So many children and young people today are starved for affection and approval; they long to hear a parent say simply, "I love you," or "I'm proud of you," or "You did a good job."

Then there are other kids who feel virtually ignored by their parents who are too preoccupied with work or other concerns to give proper attention to them. Many times, these children are so starved for love or attention that they will act out with inappropriate speech or behavior because they welcome even the negative attention of corrective discipline, regardless of the pain. Either way, whether ignored or ridden constantly by their parents, these troubled children tend to grow up with a twisted view of relationships and a negative attitude toward discipline because they see it only within the context of pain and punishment.

There certainly is a role and purpose for the rod of correction, but don't overdo it. Don't keep riding your kids, especially over minor things. Don't keep hounding them over every little detail. Give your children the freedom to make mistakes without the fear of bringing ridicule and criticism down on their heads. Making mistakes is part of the learning process. Most kids are pretty smart. They know when they've messed up, and they feel bad enough about it already without having to endure the added humiliation of parental criticism and condemnation. What they need is patience and gentle correction. If the "rod" is used sparingly, it will make more of an impression on those occasions when it *is* used. So, be judicious in its application.

The Hand Is Not a Rod

When it comes to matters of discipline, parents must walk a fine line between administering correction and committing abuse, especially in this day when corporal punishment is routinely condemned as "dangerous" by most so-called "experts" in children's health and education. Today it is more important than ever for parents to understand the basic principles governing the "rod of correction," so they can apply it safely and properly.

First of all, as I mentioned in the preceding chapter, never use your hand to punish a child. Your hand is not a rod. Never spank with your hand because you don't want your child to associate you or your hand with pain and punishment. Hands are for hugging, touching, and caressing, not inflicting physical blows. God's hands are tender, loving, and caring hands that are always

Key Note:

_____

_____

_____

_____

open to welcome us. As you seek to model the Father and His nature to your children, your hands should be used in the same way.

Instead of your hand, therefore, employ a paddle or some other instrument that will not bruise or break the skin or inflict any other kind of injury. The rod should be an instrument of love. After all, your purpose with the rod is not to hurt your child but to correct and redirect your child's behavior. The pain of a spanking, properly administered, has a way of focusing a child's mind on the matter at hand: the lesson to be learned from the experience.

Within the parameters given above, the rod can be whatever instrument you choose. In my family, as I was growing up, my father's leather belt was the rod, and it represented to us both love and pain. My brothers and sisters and I knew mom and dad loved us because they never hesitated to discipline us whenever we needed it. On those rare occasions when a belt was not readily available, such as when our dad was at work, our mom became very creative. She found something in the house to use as a rod of correction. Quite often she simply grabbed the broom and used it (the straw end, not the stick) against our backsides. The important thing is that she never used her hand and neither did my father. So we never connected our parents' hands with the pain of discipline.

Focus on the Training, Not on the Punishment

Even when punishing your children with the rod, the focus of your attention should be not on the punishment itself but on the training the punishment is intended to reinforce. Certainly, tell your children they are being punished, but don't dwell on it. Make sure they understand why they are being punished and what change in attitude or behavior is expected from them as a result.

My wife and I always did this very intentionally with our own children. Whenever either of them did something that violated the standards of our family, we sat the offender down and said something like, "I'm going to punish you, but before I do, I want to make sure you understand why, because if I don't, the punishment won't help you."

When our children were little, we bought two ping-pong paddles; one for each of them, labeled with their names. Our son's paddle was blue and our daughter's was red. And we told each of them, "This paddle is what we will use to correct you if you disobey us." They learned pretty quickly. It didn't take long before they knew as soon as we sat them down that they were going to get it, and they would start crying. We gave them some time to cry and then explained what they did wrong and why they were being punished. Then came the worst part (for them at least): we sent them to get their own paddle. As soon as they returned, we bent them over and applied the "board of education" to the "seat of learning."

Even when administering punishment, focus on training. Explain to your children the reason for the punishment or else it is nothing more than a beating that serves no purpose and accomplishes nothing except to spoil their day. As your children, they have a need and a right to know why they are being punished. Remember, this is training, not counseling. Except for older teenagers, whose reasoning abilities have matured, counseling or reasoning with children does not work because

Key Note:

_____

_____

_____

_____

they can't comprehend it; it is too abstract. Concrete things like clear directions, clear boundaries, clear rewards for right behavior, and clear penalties for wrong behavior—these are the things children understand.

Keep in mind also that spanking is done *for* a child, not *to* a child. This may sound like a narrow distinction, but it can make the difference between legitimate punishment and physical abuse. It all amounts to a difference of attitude. In the first instance, the spanking is done for the child's good; in the second, it is done to vent the parent's anger. Do you see the difference? Always discipline with the desired training objective in mind. Tell your children, "I'm doing this for your good; I'm not doing it *to* you to hurt you."

Don't Be Afraid to Let Them Cry

Don't spare the rod simply because you don't want to hear your children cry. Many parents today feel sorrier about spanking their kids than their kids do. Remember, a spanking every now and then won't kill them; even the Bible says so. (See Proverbs 23:13-14.) As a matter of fact, deep inside, your children are glad to get spanked because it proves to them that you love them; that you care enough about what they do to teach them to do the right thing. The Bible says, "*No discipline seems pleasant at the time, but painful. Later on, however, it produces a harvest of righteousness and peace for those who have been trained by it*" (Heb. 12:11 NIV).

My brothers and sisters and I are living proof of the truth of this Scripture. As I mentioned previously, there were 11 of us, and our mother and father did not spare the rod; every one of us turned out all right. So much for the "pop" psychology in the Western world that argues against any kind of physical punishment for children out of fear that it will damage them emotionally or psychologically! That philosophy certainly did not come from the Word of God.

The sad truth is that some parents go overboard with physical punishment and cross the line into abuse. But that still is no excuse for distorting and twisting the Word of God to try to adjust it to popular culture. There are those who, out of fear of the relative few who go to extremes, would force all parents by law into patterns of behavior that violate the principles of God's Word.

These biblical proverbs about the rod came from the hand and the divinely-inspired wisdom of Solomon, the third king of Israel and the wisest man who ever lived. Solomon's father was David, Israel's second king, who grew up in the hills near Bethlehem as a shepherd and the youngest son in his family. Solomon was the heir of much time-tested, "down home" wisdom that undoubtedly included understanding the benefit and value of timely and wisely administered discipline with the rod. David built a powerful kingdom and Solomon expanded it to the greatest extent it ever knew. He also built a magnificent temple for the worship of the God of Israel. It seems like David and Solomon both turned out pretty well.

Many young people and adults today who struggle with drugs or alcohol or who "shack up" with lovers or have dropped out of school or are in prison or drift from one dead-end job to another, are products of parents who "spared the rod" in favor of "counseling" their children. This approach usually fails because children who are not taught and held accountable to boundaries as children will establish no boundaries of their own

Key Note:

_____

_____

_____

_____

when they are grown, resulting in an undisciplined life with no purpose or direction. Such children, therefore, grow up unprepared for the stresses, challenges, and complexities of life.

So don't be afraid to administer the rod when needed. The Bible promises that disciplining your child with the rod will not kill him or her. Don't be afraid to watch your children cry. A little pain judiciously applied now will spare your children a world of pain later. Punish them and let them cry, but be quick also to comfort them and remind them that they still are surrounded by love.

Crying Expresses Submission

A child's crying during punishment is an expression of submission. And submission is what the disciplining parent is after. Submission does not mean breaking a child's spirit. Submission means teaching a child to willingly bring his or her will and behavior under control in respect of legitimate authority. Rather than breaking the child's will, true submission involves the child's will being brought under deliberate control. But children must be taught this; it does not come naturally. Childhood is the time for teaching submission, and for forcing it when necessary, so that when children grow up, they will choose submission on their own when appropriate.

I visit and minister in prisons on occasion and one thing I have noticed is how many of the inmates are sharp-looking, handsome fellows. On some of these visits I have even seen guys I went to school with. All of those men are in prison because they made a mistake of some kind and violated the law. As I have watched them, the thought has occurred to me, "Now they are being parented by people in uniform." Just like children, they are told when to get up, when to go to bed, where to work, when to work, how long to work, what to do, what not to do, when to eat, and when to go to the bathroom. Their whole life is regulated by forced parenting. Why? Because they weren't properly parented while they were children, which is one reason they ended up in prison. Your children either will be parented by you now or by someone else later. Either you do it or the government will.

I asked many of those men how they felt about what they did, and every one of them expressed regret over what they did. They wished they weren't incarcerated. Some of them even started crying. Why? Because they finally had someone to whom they had to submit: the penal system.

So don't be afraid to see your children cry during correction. Correction is a necessary part of the process of restoring them to the right path and the right values and right behavior. A little crying is not a bad thing. God wants tender hearts, not hard hearts. When people cry, it means that their hearts are tender.

Spanking Ministers to the Whole Person

Sometimes we assume that when we spank our children, we are administering discipline to their physical bodies only. In truth, corporal punishment goes far beyond the physical in its benefit and effectiveness. Like all human beings, children are a unity of body, soul, and spirit. The objective of training and of corporal punishment is to get the corrective lesson into their spirits. There is a particular way they should walk and since they have stepped out of that way they are going to receive a corrective action to set them on the right path again.

This is why it is important for us to explain to our children why they are being punished. With the help of the rod, our

Key Note:

_____

_____

_____

_____

words reach into their spirits and the Lord can correct the wrong thoughts and attitudes in their hearts, which will lead to altered and corrected behavior. The rod is an instrument that helps children change their minds from the wrong to the right.

The Bible says that as a man thinks in his heart, so is he. (See Proverbs 23:7.) In this context, the heart really means the mind, so the use of the rod is tied to the heart—to the very root and center of a child's personality and being. Administration of the rod penetrates to the heart of a child's very identity. It therefore contains the potential power to effect change in the child's life and behavior. So all of childhood training, including the use of the rod, must be focused on the heart of the child and not just on the child's physical body.

The Rod Drives Out Foolishness

The rod of correction is important in the life of a child also because it plays a major role in bringing the child to maturity by driving out foolishness. Scripture supports this idea: *"Foolishness is bound up in the heart of a child; The rod of correction will drive it far from him"* (Prov. 22:15 NKJV). Note what this verse does not say. It never says our explanations or our discussions or our counseling with our children will drive foolishness away from them. It says the rod will drive it away.

Foolishness is bound up in the hearts of children. Part of this is their natural immaturity. But foolishness that lingers in the heart after a child has passed into the teen years and adulthood is sure to cause trouble. We all have seen adults who, regardless of their chronological age, seem never to have grown up. In almost every circumstance, that fact causes ongoing problems for them and their families. A child left to himself will grow like a wild bush and eventually be out of control. The rod of correction will help prune and shape and guide that wildness (not destroy it or remove it completely) so that the child still has spirit and will and determination and the potential for greatness, but all of these are under conscious control and focused in the right direction.

You've got to train and prune and guide a plant if you want it to be fully cultivated. Cultivation is the difference between having a garden and having chaos. No garden grows automatically. Even Adam had to work to dress and keep the Garden of Eden. (See Genesis 2:15.) Cultivating a garden takes hard work. You have to plant it, fertilize it, irrigate it, weed it, prune it, and keep the bugs away. Only then can you hope to have a fruitful harvest.

Children must be cultivated with the same kind of care and attention; otherwise, they will grow wild. Discipline is an indispensable part of the cultivation process. And just as you sometimes have to take a spade and a hoe to resistant soil in a garden, you sometimes have to apply the rod of correction to the resistant "soil" of a child's mind and heart and character, softening and weeding them so they will become responsive to the right influences. Spare not the rod if you want to bring up happy, confident, well-adjusted children of godly character.

Key Note:

_____

_____

_____

_____

Chapter 5

In Wisdom, Stature, and Favor

By Myles Munroe

How important is parenting? It's important enough that God incorporated it into His plan for humanity and human procreation from the beginning. God was not locked into any particular way of doing things. He could have chosen any means for populating the earth with humans, but He chose the process of sexual reproduction with parents conceiving, birthing, and training their children.

How important is parenting? Important enough that God the Father chose to send His Son to earth as a human child entrusted to the care and rearing of human parents. Children are not designed to raise themselves, and the Son of God on earth was no exception. Jesus needed the care and attention of loving parents in order to grow into the man He was supposed to be.

If we are looking for a model of effective parenting to use in becoming better parents ourselves, we can find no better example than that of Mary and Joseph's parenting of Jesus. Although

Key Note:

_____

_____

_____

_____

the Bible contains no specific references or examples of their parenting "technique," we can learn a great deal by studying the outcome of their parenting: the man Jesus became under their guidance.

The New Testament provides very little information about Jesus prior to His manhood and the beginning of His public ministry. In fact, the Gospels of Matthew and Luke are the only books in the Bible that mention anything at all about Jesus' formative years. While both books relate events surrounding Jesus' birth and infancy, only Luke tells us anything about His childhood, and that is limited to one event that occurred when Jesus was 12 years old. But that one account contains valuable information and guidance to help parents raise their children well.

His parents went to Jerusalem every year at the Feast of the Passover. And when He was twelve years old, they went up to Jerusalem according to the custom of the feast. When they had finished the days, as they returned, the Boy Jesus lingered behind in Jerusalem. And Joseph and His mother did not know it; but supposing Him to have been in the company, they went a day's journey, and sought Him among their relatives and acquaintances. So when they did not find Him, they returned to Jerusalem, seeking Him. Now so it was that after three days they found Him in the temple, sitting in the midst of the teachers, both listening to them and asking them questions. And all who heard Him were astonished at His understanding and answers. So when they saw Him, they were amazed; and His mother said to Him, "Son, why have You done this to us? Look, Your father and I have sought You anxiously."

And He said to them, "Why did you seek Me? Did you not know that I must be about My Father's business?" But they did not understand the statement which He spoke to them.

Then He went down with them and came to Nazareth, and was subject to them, but His mother kept all these things in her heart. And Jesus increased in wisdom and stature, and in favor with God and men (Luke 2:41-52 NKJV).

Every year Jesus' parents went to Jerusalem for the Passover, which shows that Mary and Joseph were faithful, regular, and consistent in their worship of God. And they taught Jesus to be the same. This is obvious by Jesus' demeanor and behavior. Twelve was the age at which a Jewish male made the passage from boyhood to manhood and began to focus specifically on preparing to follow in his father's footsteps. In Jesus' case this meant being apprenticed to His earthly father, Joseph, in the carpenter shop. But, as this story indicates, Jesus at 12 was already preparing to walk in the footsteps of His true Father in Heaven.

When Jesus stayed behind in the Temple after His parents started home, He astounded the rabbis and learned scholars there with His insight and understanding—evidence of good teaching at home. The fact that Jesus listened and asked questions reveals that He also knew how to show proper respect and honor to His elders—another quality He undoubtedly learned from His parents.

Another evidence of Mary and Joseph's good parenting is the confidence and respect with which Jesus replied to their anxious question upon finding Him after three days of searching:

Key Note:

_____

_____

_____

_____

"Why did you seek Me? Did you not know that I must be about My Father's business?" Mary and Joseph were preparing Jesus for His mission in life and had done a good job.

Most significant of all, however, is the information contained in the final paragraph of this passage. First, Jesus went home to Nazareth with Mary and Joseph and was "subject" to them. The Son of God and Lord of creation willingly made Himself subject to the training and authority of His human parents. Second, *"Jesus increased in wisdom and stature, and in favor with God and men."* This final statement reveals four areas of emphasis where Mary and Joseph focused their training of Jesus. As such it also presents a guideline for where parents today should place their focus.

Wisdom

On the road to maturity Jesus grew in four areas: wisdom, stature, favor with God, and favor with man. It is no accident that wisdom is listed first. Wisdom is God's first priority for His children. Therefore, imparting wisdom to our children should be our first priority as parents. What is wisdom? Wisdom is the application of God's Word to daily life. In other words, the number-one thing we need to teach our children is how to eat properly, not just physical food, but the spiritual food of the Word of God.

It is never too early to begin bringing our children into contact with God's Word. We can start even before they are born. Studies have proven conclusively that unborn children can hear and respond to aural stimuli. Read the Bible aloud over your children while they are still in the womb. Play praise and worship music as well as sacred classical music. Start filling their ears (and therefore their minds) with the truth of God's Word before they are born into this world that is filled with the devil's lies.

Remember that spirits are ageless. Our physical bodies age but not our spirits. So the spirit of a child (even an unborn child) can receive the living Word. Jesus said, "...*The words that I speak to you are spirit, and they are life*" (John 6:63 NKJV). When we offer a child the spiritual food of God's Word, we can feed his or her spirit even while that child is still in the womb.

Jesus in the Temple in Jerusalem at the age of 12 displayed wisdom beyond His years. One telltale sign of wisdom is the ability to apply knowledge, and the most basic way of applying knowledge is by asking questions. Jesus knew the Word of God well enough to ask astute questions of the scholars and teachers and to give perceptive answers, enough so that they were "*astonished at His understanding and answers*." Part of this was due, no doubt, to the fact that He was the Son of God. But the lion's share of the credit must go to His earthly parents, Mary and Joseph, who patiently and faithfully and continually imparted wisdom to Him, teaching Him to know and apply God's Word. God the Father had entrusted His Son to their care and they proved faithful to that trust.

Studies in child development and psychology have revealed that the pattern of a child's life is generally set by age four. This means that whatever a child learns in the first four years of life will determine the course of the rest of his life: how he thinks, feels, talks, and acts. Everything else is just reinforcement. This is why it is so important to get the Word of God into a child's spirit from the earliest possible moments of life. Which would you rather: that the pattern of your children's lives be set by the Spirit of God or by the spirit of the world? The world bombards

Key Note:

_____

_____

_____

our children constantly with its own twisted values and distorted view of morality. As parents, we need to be just as diligent—or even more so—in bombarding them with the wisdom of the Word of God. And it needs to start when they are small children. Waiting until they get to high school is too late; the pattern of their lives will already be set by then.

One of the things that my wife and I did with our own children was to instruct them to read the "wisdom" books of the Bible—the Psalms, Proverbs, and Ecclesiastes—over and over again as part of our daily family devotionals. Each day one of them would read one chapter out loud. Over time, the words of Scripture sink below the conscious level into the subconscious and into the spirit, where they effect change from the inside out.

Everything we need to know for practical, godly living is found in the Psalms, Proverbs, and Ecclesiastes. Everything else is reinforcement. The Book of Psalms contains many prophecies about the Messiah and the Resurrection and the redemption work of God, so by reading the Psalms we learn about redemption. In the Book of Proverbs we find God's principles and laws for success, happiness, and fruitfulness in life. The Book of Proverbs also talks more about parenting than any other book of the Bible. The Book of Ecclesiastes describes in vivid detail the futility and emptiness of trying to live without God.

Parents, focus your primary attention on imparting wisdom and the Word of God to your children, especially while they are very young. This should be your highest priority.

Stature

The second thing parents must focus on is developing their children's stature. Stature has to do with physical characteristics such as height and build, but it also has to do more broadly with overall physical development, particularly discipline. In this case, not discipline as in punishment, but discipline in behavior and manner; in other words, self-control.

Luke 2:52 says that Jesus increased in stature, which means He grew physically. But He also grew in physical discipline. Verse 51 says that Jesus was subject to His earthly parents; He submitted willingly to their guidance and training, and through them He learned self-control.

Children do not exercise self-control by nature. Until they are taught otherwise, they will say whatever is on their mind, seek to gratify every desire without discrimination, and insist that the world revolves around them. We have to teach our children how to keep their legs crossed, how to keep their zippers up, how to restrict and control their emotions and their sexual passions, and how to protect themselves from the temptations of tobacco, alcohol, and drugs. We must teach them the importance of honesty and of telling the truth and of treating other people with fairness, kindness, and generosity.

As a child, Jesus was no different. He developed in the same way that any other child does. Although Jesus was the Son of God, He also was 100 percent human, with all the urges, passions, and desires that are natural for human beings. Like anyone else, Jesus had to learn to control His sex drive. He had to learn to subordinate His own needs and desires for those of others. He had to learn the Word of God and the proper way to worship God. Sometimes we assume that because Jesus was the Son of God He was able to take shortcuts to maturity. That is not the case.

Jesus was just like us in every way, except that He was without sin. He experienced the same temptations and frustrations

Key Note:

_____

_____

_____

_____

we do. He got hot and cold and became weary and needed sleep just like we do.

If Jesus needed to learn all these things, then certainly our children do. So many adults today are in prison or have wrecked, disorderly, or disorganized lives because they never learned discipline as children. And they never learned discipline because their parents never taught them. No matter what their height, they are, therefore, persons of diminished stature.

Wisdom is the first priority, because it is necessary for helping children develop the stature of discipline. The two must go together to bring children to full maturity. Wisdom without discipline leads to wasted knowledge, while discipline without wisdom leads to wasted effort. What good is wisdom if you don't know how to focus your priorities? What use is discipline if you don't know how or where to apply it?

Favor With God

The third area of focus for parents to concentrate on is raising children to know and receive God's favor. In other words, parents, we need to teach our children to develop a personal relationship with God. As I said before, most children are visual learners; they learn best by observation. This means that if they are going to develop a personal relationship with God, they will need to see it modeled by their parents. Don't expect your kids to read the Bible if they don't see you reading the Bible. Don't expect your kids to pray if they don't see and hear you pray. Don't expect your kids to value the church and the community of faith if they don't see you valuing them. Don't expect your kids to trust God in the daily affairs of life if they don't see you trusting Him daily. Don't expect your kids to love the Lord if they don't see that you love Him. Don't expect your kids to give the things of God top priority in their lives if they don't see you doing so.

Can young children truly have a serious relationship with God? Absolutely. Jesus did by the time He was 12, and probably long before. I was serious about God when I was 13. Remember, the spirit is ageless; children can relate to God through their spirits in a way that is just as real for them as is the relationship with God that adults enjoy. Train your children from a very early age to love and trust God. Teach them by example how to live a life of faith. Studies bear out the sobering fact that most people who do not turn to the Lord while they are children never do. Don't neglect and don't delay teaching your children to know and love God; their eternal destiny depends on it.

Favor With Man

Fourth and finally, parents need to focus on raising their children to live in favor with other people. This does not mean teaching them to become "man-pleasers," but it means that you make sure they know the social graces and the basic principles of living responsibly. Children need to know how to get along with other people, and the place to learn these things is at home. It is not the job of daycare workers to teach these principles. It is not the job of the schools to teach them either. It is not the job of a babysitter or a nanny to teach these principles to your children. It is your job to teach them.

Where do you think Jesus learned how to talk to people respectfully? Where did He learn compassion for the poor and the sick? Where did He learn how to build good relationships? Jesus learned these things at home by being in submission to His earthly parents. Joseph and Mary obviously had that kind of spirit in them, which is one reason why God the Father chose them to be the earthly guardians of His Son. He needed people who could model love and compassion and kindness and positive relationship-building.

What are your children learning from you? Are they learning to be kind because they see you being kind? Are they learning to value strong and lasting relationships because that is the kind of relationships you build? Are they developing compassionate hearts because they see the compassion in yours? Are they developing a generous, giving spirit because they see your generosity on a regular basis? Do they care about the poor because you care about the poor? Are they learning social and cultural responsibility because you live responsibly in those areas? Always remember that your children are watching you. They want to be like you and will take their cues from you. Since your kids will very likely turn out to be just like you, make sure you live like the kind of person you want them to be.

Parenting is all about teaching children to love and live for God and training them how to behave properly in society and live as responsible citizens. These are things to be learned at home. Modern society has developed a lot of off-base, alternative ideas and theories for raising children, but in the end it all comes back to one inescapable truth: *There is no substitute for parental influence in the lives of children.*

No one in the world is better equipped than parents to teach children the four essential qualities of wisdom, discipline (self-control), relating rightly to God, and living rightly in society. These are the cornerstones for success in life; the practical working out in day-to-day living of what Jesus identified as the two greatest commandments: "*You shall love the Lord your God with all your heart, with all your soul, and with all your mind*" (Matt. 22:37 NKJV); and, "*You shall love your neighbor as yourself*" (Matt. 22:39 NKJV). Children must learn these things at home before they can live them in society. But once they learn them they will be ready for anything life can throw at them. Once their parents have shown them the way, children will not turn away from it when they are old. They will be God's kids for life.

PART II

Building Relationships

By David Burrows

Chapter 6

A BETTER TOMORROW

BY DAVID BURROWS

In order to create a brighter future for your child and yourself, it is important to recognize the importance of becoming the best possible parent and to act upon this goal as early as possible. If you don't start early, you may have to face some of the greatest and most disheartening challenges imaginable. It is what I call the "too-late syndrome," and, as a counselor and pastor, I've seen it happen far too often.

Here is what frequently happens: The parents of a teenager arrive in my office and tell me that they face an overwhelming situation regarding their son or daughter, who has done or is doing something that is causing great grief and tribulation for the family. The child might be taking drugs, behaving in unruly ways, or refusing to submit to any instructions from the parents. Then parents ask, "How did this happen?"

It may be too late to find an answer to this question, but it is not too late to find a solution. Sometimes, unfortunately, it is too late to find an immediate solution, because the child is already

Key Note:

_____

_____

_____

_____

hopelessly involved in the problematic behavior. In most cases, when parents finally recognize their child has a problem, that problem has already been developing for several years. How do you avoid the "too-late syndrome"? Start early.

Get the proper information about raising children and dealing with teenagers on a before-needed basis rather than a too-late reaction. This means we need to be vigilant and diligent in our role as parents. We need to obtain the necessary information and guidance before a problematic situation occurs rather than trying to play catch-up afterward.

Too often parents have read no books, attended no seminars, and have studied nothing that would enable them or prepare them to successfully deal with parenting issues. Therefore when problems arise, they are not equipped to handle situations—especially concerning teens.

At times I require parents to read a godly parenting book or listen to a teaching tape before seeing me a second time. Although some are irritated to have "homework," nonetheless, I believe it is important that parents seek understanding, especially from the Bible, that will provide them with the information to help them, and may answer their questions. Parents must take the time to invest in their family's future. Some sacrifices are necessary to correct a situation that has been forming for years. Fortunately, a number of parents have accepted the "homework" challenge and often come back to my office and report that the information was extremely helpful to them.

It is interesting to note that in order to obtain a driver's license certain requirements must be met. There are certain things you must know before you are permitted to drive a vehicle on the road. You must study driving manuals, take a test, and if you pass, you receive a license and are legally permitted to drive.

Unfortunately, being a parent does not have similar requirements. It's on-the-job training for parents. That's why it is important to seek the right information *before* we become a parent if we are to be successful in that role. You need information about the stages of life and development of children that will help you to better understand and deal with each circumstance and challenge that arises.

It's crucial to know about the changes that take place in the lives of our children as they grow so we will be able to deal with each stage correctly. Through study, you learn that you do not deal with a young child in the same way that you deal with a teen. A child is different from a teenager. There are various issues that develop between the childhood years and teenage years that a parent must be aware of and prepare for. Teenagers are rapidly changing creatures, and having advance knowledge about what to expect will help us prepare for and know how to deal with the inevitable challenges these changes present to us and our teens. It is important to prepare for the challenges you will face with your teens before you enter the "too-late zone."

A brighter tomorrow for parents and teens begins today. Godly knowledge and information will create an enjoyable family future. Never wait until you face a problem to prepare for it. Since there is no school for parenting, each parent must make it a point to gain the information they need for themselves. Read books, attend seminars, and buy tapes, CDs, or DVDs, join a church parenting group. Prepare yourself for the inevitable. The potential gap that may develop between parents and their children is bridged with information and understanding.

Key Note:

_____

_____

_____

_____

In the same way that parents must prepare, it is important for teens to understand what to expect during their adolescence, as well. Encourage them to read about the teen years before they get there; by doing so, they will learn from the successes and mistakes of others. And you will, too, as you try to understand what those years involve. While it is important to have fun, and there is nothing wrong with having fun, it is also important to protect yourself from making harmful mistakes. Basic biblical commands, such as: "*Honor your father and mother*" or "*Listen to your father's instruction,*" are principles that should not be forgotten. They preserve life and add peace to our days.

Chapter 7

THE ORIGINAL PLAN

BY DAVID BURROWS

> *[Children] are a heritage from the LORD, children a reward from him. ...Blessed is the [parent] whose quiver is full of them. They will not be put to shame when they contend with their enemies in the gate* (Psalm 127:3-5 NIV).

Back to the Original?

*I*n life there are originals, imitations, spin-offs, and "knock-offs". However, if you want the best, you have to go back to the original. When we discover what the original design for the family is, there is where we must set our foundation. The family was designed to be the primary institution—the cornerstone—of society. It is the foundation upon which society is to be built.

What we have today, in many cases, is not the original. What we have today is a confused concept of family life. No matter how prominent or accepted these new family "arrangements" may be, the result is still widespread confusion.

Key Note:

_____

_____

_____

_____

Political Correctness

I make no attempt to be politically correct or to appease a particular segment of the population—rather, I am attempting to find solutions for the problems that are faced by many parents, teens, and families in our society today. In order to do this, I have to explain the situation from my perspective. I have worked in this arena for many years as a pastor, counselor, author, teacher, preacher, advisor, and victim; therefore, I know that I am well qualified to speak authoritatively on this vitally important subject.

One of the most bizarre situations I have come across in recent times was a story about a young woman who became a member of a male college football team. She later reported that she had been groped and molested by her teammates. When I heard the story, I thought, "Why would leaders and coaches put a female among 40 or more males on a team, and expect the young men who are full of testosterone to ignore their female teammate?" This is swinging the door to temptation and abuse open wide. What is the point of having a female on a male team in the first place? Women have the potential to perform as men do; but they are not men, so why put females on a male team? The "logic" we see exhibited in today's world is sometimes hard to understand.

While I recognize the confusion that exists in a "politically correct" environment, I believe we have to develop strategies that work within the context of the times in which we live. We must work with the situation as it is, while still promoting the ideal family and the original concept of family life. We can never allow our focus to be taken off of God's original plan for the family, no matter how confused it may become in our world. We must remember that children and teens are victims of the confusion that exists, and they are not the creators of it.

In light of this, we have to determine what we can do to work with teens who come from broken and confused family structures and help them learn how to survive and cope. At the same time, we must teach them about God's ideal of family life and reinforce the values that are associated with His ideal.

Championing God's Plan

What is His original plan? Let's begin by looking at the roles of each member of the family. What should a parent be doing? What should a child be doing? What was God's purpose and design for parents and children, particularly teenagers and young adults? As we continue, let's deal with the nature and role of each.

The original plan involves God as the ultimate authority (the BIG Chief)—He is our Heavenly Father. The human father is the head of the family. (This does not mean that he is always the smartest or best member of the family, but someone has to be in charge; otherwise, we have a two-headed monster in the family!)

The father is similar to the plant manager in a company. The mother is his assistant (even though she may be more qualified than the man) who makes sure the plant is managed well, based upon her unique design and role for service in this capacity.

The children are the like the workers, who will one day become managers as a result of the information, instruction, and interaction they experience with their authority figures. Children are supposed to learn everything about life from their parents—proper rules, roles, and behaviors. They also learn to

Key Note:

_____

_____

_____

_____

formulate dreams and visions for their own lives based on their parent's examples.

It is a fact of life that, regardless of feelings or sentiments, parents out-rank their children. Every army has its privates, generals, lieutenants, sergeants, and so on. Like an army, the family must have a proper chain-of-command to successfully accomplish goals. God (the Commander-in-Chief) has appointed parents to be the "generals" in a family. This does not mean, however, that parents are always right, nor does it mean that they are right even 90 percent of the time. It just means that they occupy the top position in the family, and God always works through proper authority, good organization, and order.

As we go forward, we must realize that the changing face of the family means that great adjustments, opportunities, and challenges have to be dealt with. As parents, it is important to renew our commitment to God's plan, no matter what the situation we find ourselves. We must take every opportunity to champion God's plan, no matter what the world says or does.

The world seeks to change the original in order to accommodate the current mess rather than acknowledge the turmoil and return to the original. If God is the Creator (if He isn't, then we are all accidents with no purpose, so whatever we do is left up to our own imaginations), then His plan is the one we should seek to follow, because the Creator knows how His creation should work.

This reminds me of a story about a young boy who was being disruptive in a church meeting. His parents wanted to quiet him, so they looked for a task that would take him a long time to complete. They found a puzzle that represented the globe; they scrambled the pieces of the puzzle, thinking it would take hours for the boy to figure it out and put the pieces together.

They left him in the next room with the puzzle, feeling certain that they would not be disturbed again. Within a few minutes of resuming their meeting, however, there was knock on the door and the little boy entered gleefully and expressed how he had already solved the puzzle.

When his parents returned to the room with him, they looked in astonishment as the young man showed them the completed puzzle! In fact, they were so astonished that they asked him how he had accomplished it so quickly.

The boy said, "On the back side of the puzzle there was a man's picture. I put the man together. When I put the man together, the world came together!"

This beautiful story illustrates my point clearly. If the man is together, the family will come together; if the family becomes a tighter unit, the community will come together; if the community comes together, society will come together; if society comes together, the nation will come together; if the nation comes together, the world will come together. It all begins with the original plan for the family, a plan that began with one man and one woman.

Children are commanded by their Commander-in-Chief to obey their parents. "*Children, obey your parents in the Lord, for this is right*" (Eph. 6:1). Children are commanded to obey their parents "*in the Lord.*" Not all parents are "in the Lord," but children should endeavor to obey, except in severe circumstances such as acting outside the law or in cases of abuse.

The Bible notes that parents should not provoke their children. Paul writes, "*Fathers, do not provoke your children, lest they*

Key Note:

_____

_____

_____

_____

become discouraged" (Col. 3:21 NKJV). Neither should parents cause their children to go against established authority. We will deal with this subject a little more as we continue, but the principle is that parents are higher in rank than their children and even where there is a lack of respect for the person, the position of parent must still be respected. We have now established what the original plan is, but that still leads us to the question of how do we create and build better parent, teen, and family relationships? It all begins with understanding!

Chapter 8

UNDERSTANDING TEENS

BY DAVID BURROWS

The remainder of the book emphasizes the challenges of raising teenagers. Although your children may be infants, toddlers, or elementary schoolers now—they will be teens faster than you can even imagine. Continuing to read will give you insights that will save you from "too-late" syndrome later in life and the wisdom nuggets will prepare you for the inevitable.

It is a challenging and awakening time for most parents when their children become teenagers. Their precious children, who were once so obedient, lovable, sociable, and attached to them suddenly change as they become teenagers. Most parents are shocked—but should they be? This same phenomenon happens every generation, and should be anticipated.

Many parents say, "How can I deal with such an unpredictable teen? She used to be so sweet. Now all we do is argue and fight!" At one time the young lady thought the world of her mother, but now she doesn't want mommy to take her to certain events or pick her up from a party. She no longer agrees with

---

Key Note:

_____

_____

_____

her mother's view of the world. She expresses opinions that are different from her parents on many critical issues, and her interests change to the point where both parents and teenager seem to be going in completely different directions.

How can we understand teens? We must begin by taking a look at their makeup—their characteristics, values, and behaviors.

The Teenage Nature

1. Teens desire their own identity.

Parents enjoy having their child believe everything they say, look up to them for advice, and tell them everything that happens in school. But parents get one of the biggest shocks of life when little Susie or Johnny reaches the age of 13, and all of a sudden their blue skies turn green! Your daughter comes home and says, "You know what, mom, I believe the sky is green." Or your son may say, "I don't see why I can't have sex if I want to." They may ask why they have to go to church, "How do you know that God really exists?" or "What's wrong with listening to a rock band?" When these things happen, mom and dad are shocked, and the "war" is on.

Fact: All teens want to establish their own identity—they want to form their own ideas, apart from their parents.

This is a very natural and logical process for a young person to go through. The process is called individuation. Life consists of stages, and each stage, after completed, leads to the next. Often there are physical changes that go along with the psychological and social changes. With the onset of puberty, the acute awareness of sexuality begins, so the teen begins to ask questions about sex and have feelings and thoughts they never had before.

Parents already have their individual identities. They have already gone through the process of individuation. If they handle the situation properly, parents can help their kids find answers to their questions and help their children form their proper identities. However, if this is handled incorrectly, it can mean disaster. The lines of communication may break down and replaced with a defensive wall that may remain in place for years.

If a child says, "Don't drop me off at school; I can take care of myself," he or she is not necessarily taking a stand against his or her parents. The teen is actually saying, "I want to be more responsible for my own affairs and I want to identify with my peers." So don't take such comments personally.

2. Teens develop their own language and culture.

It was not very long ago when most parents of teenagers were teens themselves and they spoke a language that was "in" for that time. However, today's teenagers' language and culture is very different and many parents are out of touch. Parents tend to forget what they went through and wonder why their teens have to have their own language, music, and culture. In every generation, the new culture is seen as being more bizarre than the previous one.

Parents must contend with new words and phrases that are already set in today's teen world and culture. A teenager's slang may consist of words his or her parents have not heard before; therefore, the parents don't understand the meanings. Sometimes words may even reappear with new meanings even if they are the same words that the parents grew up with. In most cases, however, many of these words and phrases have a new twist. The Internet has harvested a huge new crop of words that teens are more aware of than their parents. This is also true of

Key Note:

_____

_____

_____

_____

music. The differing musical tastes of teens and their parents can cause problems between them. One generation's music may be just noise to another generation. And this works both ways. The "language barrier" frequently blocks the communication between parents and teens.

Another aspect of teen culture involves hairstyles. Years ago, house wars began when a teen came home with shoulder-length hair or an Afro. Parents just didn't understand. Now guys may wear ponytails, earrings, weird haircuts, tattoos, and other fashions that are often just statements of independence and changing styles. We must face one thing: Most teens think their parents are "un-cool" or "out of touch." Usually parents don't have time (or take the time) to figure out or understand the latest fashion trends, music styles, or cultural phenomena, so they are "out of touch."

3. Teenagers are idealistic.

Teens are full of idealism. This is true of every generation of teenagers. Teens believe they can change the world and that they have new ideas that are different and better than those of their parents. Teens look for a better existence and are critical of existing institutions. They proudly proclaim and believe, "We can make it better (do it better, make a change)."

Throughout much of modern history, when the younger generation thought that something was wrong with the existing society and its institutions, they felt they could change it and make it better. Every new generation of young people sees new ideas, new ways, and new approaches to problems. That young people want to try to change the world will always be a part of the human experience. The fact is that many of the most creative inventions came from younger minds. For example, the personal computer was developed by two college dropouts. And many college students became rich by applying technology to the needs of modern society. The idealism of young people is often a benefit to society, as long as the idealism remains within the realm of positive creativity.

4. Teens are full of energy.

Most teens are full of unbridled energy. They always want to know "What's happening? Where's the party? Where can we go to have a good time?"

The fact that teens are full of energy does not have to be a negative factor in the relationship between parents and teens. It is simply a part of life. But, if this energy is not channeled in the right direction, it can become negative and very destructive. Kids have to be busy; therefore, parents must provide opportunities for them to keep busy doing the right kinds of things. Teens want and need positive activities into which they can channel their energy. That is why it is vitally important for adults to invest their time in teens to make sure they play or party in safe environments. It is an adult's responsibility to be certain that teenagers have positive programs and activities in which to be involved; otherwise, they could be misguided into destructive behaviors.

It is wrong to expect a teenager not to want to have fun, play, and expend their seemingly inexhaustible supply of energy. The teen years are naturally a stage of development that is full of energy.

5. Teens often rebel and question.

Conflict between teens and parents are inevitable when a youth begins to question and challenge the way things are. No institution is safe from the questions of youth.

Key Note:

_____

_____

_____

_____

Let's take school for example. A teenager might ask, "Why do I have to go to school?" Or say, "I don't believe this history stuff; they are just trying to brainwash us."

Another institution a youth might question is the church. A teenager might ask, "How do I know God really exists?" Or "There are so many religions; which one is real?" They may say, "I don't believe this God stuff just because you do, Dad."

Concerning government and politics, a youth might say, "All these politicians are just crooks and clowns; they're lying to us. They need to be tossed out!" Or: "Maybe this capitalist democracy stuff is wrong. Maybe communism or socialism is better."

Usually parents have already settled these issues for themselves. Since they probably went through similar questioning some years before, they have fewer questions than their teenager. But this questioning and challenging of institutions and authority needs to be handled correctly by the parent. As painful as it may be, parents, and society as a whole, need to answer a teenager's questions honestly and not force their opinions. Let teens determine for themselves what truth is; adults should just provide the best information possible.

6. Teens take chances.

Young people may blurt out their feelings and do things before thinking them through or considering the consequences. They will often experiment with many things, including limits and boundaries. They want to go "where no man has gone before" and check out "the final frontier." Many times teens do things they later regret. In many cases they are experimenting with things their parents have already tried.

It is interesting to note that adults will speak to children about things they themselves have already been through, and then their kids, after listening to them, will go out and experiment with the very same things! Over and over again I have talked to young people about my troubled and destructive life when I was on drugs and the time I spent on the street; yet they turn around and do the very same things. One high school student said to me, "You had your time; it's our time now." The sentiment he was expressing could be put like this, "It's my time to experiment, to take some chances."

Unfortunately, taking chances can lead to prison, death, or physical harm. As adults, we must provide everything we can to minimize the opportunities for teens to take chances and make wrong choices. It is important to *create an environment of accountability* in which the teenagers know you are involved in their lives and that you are trying to help them avoid the consequences of bad decisions. Keep asking questions without being overbearing.

7. Teens have respect for truth.

A song that was popular a few years ago said, "Everybody's searching for a hero, someone to look up to." Today's youth, like those before, are searching for someone to look up to. They don't like hypocrites; they are looking for adults who live by enduring principles, whether they agree or disagree with those principles.

Believe it or not, kids cry out for discipline, direction, and purpose. They look up to and respect adults who have strong moral convictions. And adults who care enough about them to keep them from destroying themselves. Teens also look up to other teens who they perceive to be strong in their convictions—whether right or wrong. Truth from the pages of the most

Key Note:

_____

_____

_____

_____

important Book in the world and from the lives of those who know it is something many youths are crying for. Even while teenagers try to throw off restraint, most realize that there are right and wrong behaviors, and they would ultimately like to behave the right way even though it may not appear that way at times.

One of the most interesting conversations I have ever had was with a young man who appeared not to be interested in doing anything but things that were wrong. I asked him if he believed in God and if he wanted to do what was right. He said that he wanted to do right, but he watched his mother go to church every week and talk about God and then come home and curse him out! This caused the young man to take a backseat approach to God and observe others, to see if they were hypocrites.

8. Teens are great collaborators.

Peer pressure is a fact of teenage life. Teenagers experience gratification from impressing each other and from "beating the system." Teens often plan together. If they intend to sneak off for the night or go to a party they are not supposed to attend, they will plan to share the consequences together or try and beat the system together. Teens hardly ever do anything that is not designed to impress their peers.

Parents, on the other hand, are different. They do not usually collaborate with their peers when they are dealing with children, but children will collaborate with each other when they are dealing with their parents. It is critical for parents to recognize and be aware of the collaboration that takes place among teens.

Remember, Parents

Teens are:
Idealistic
Energetic

Chance-takers
Identity-seekers
Collaborators
Truth-seekers
Sometimes rebellious
Living in their own culture
Using their own language.

In light of these characteristics, you can help your teenagers through these exciting and challenging years by:

1. Communicating. Don't use one-way communication with them; instead, develop two-way communication.
2. Listening and understanding.
3. Preparing them for the future.
4. Encouraging them.
5. Disciplining them.
6. Caring for and about them.
7. Not provoking them.
8. Giving them unconditional love.

Key Note:

_____

_____

_____

_____

Chapter 9

UNDERSTANDING PARENTS

BY DAVID BURROWS

*U*nderstanding us—parents—can be just as frustrating for teenagers as it is for parents to understand teenagers. Recognizing our strengths and weaknesses can help bridge the generation gap. Have your teen (or pre-teen) read this chapter. Or better yet, read it together!

A Parent's Nature

1. Parents are wise.

In most cases, parents have accumulated wisdom over the years. Their life experiences have taught them many things which help them know and understand certain things. There was a weekly television show several years ago titled, "Father Knows Best," suggesting that parents have acquired "some" wisdom through the years.

Most parents have already experienced what you are going through, and have gained wisdom from the "school of hard knocks." Yes, your parents are wise because they have experienced

Key Note:

_____

_____

_____

_____

the things you have; they remember what they went through, and very frequently they know your story before you finish telling it.

Because of those past experiences, most parents can figure some things out and see the train (wreck) coming long before it arrives. For example, many parents have gone through teen pregnancy, drug abuse, wild partying, and irresponsible living, so they have collected memories over the years, and they most likely recall those experiences when they hear you talking the same things. This is also the reason many overreact—they don't want you to make the same mistakes.

2. Parents are realists.

A parent may say something like, "Son, you might as well get used to it; the world isn't going to change. I tried that before." Parents tend to think in realistic terms. They went through their own period of idealism and became resigned to what they consider the "realities of life." They know certain things never or hardly ever change, and that time is better spent on something else.

Parents tend to view things realistically and base their judgments on what has happened before. You may have a great idea, but your parent may say, "That's not going to work" or "That's impractical." They tend to see the difficulties rather than the possibilities.

Realism is part of adult life. Working nine to five, paying bills, and caring for children can cause a serious dose of reality to set in. When you don't have bills to pay or other responsibilities to take care of, you can dream all day and think of possibilities and be idealistic. The grind of everyday adult life, however, can temper idealism and cause it to turn to realism.

3. Parents are practical.

Parents normally are inclined to calculate the risks and rewards and to determine what's most practical before making a decision. A young person, on the other hand, will often act first and worry about the consequences later.

Parents do just the opposite. They think first and proceed cautiously. If something appears uncertain or too risky, a parent will, in most cases, tell you not to proceed. Sometimes that is good. At other times, however, it may actually rob a teen of an opportunity. Nevertheless, this approach is simply a part of parent's makeup. The first question a parent will normally ask is, "How much is this going to cost?" This question is born out of their having to deal with the cost of living, paying bills, and balancing the budget.

4. Parents are usually settled.

When parents were much younger, they did the same things you like to do. Some of today's parents were activists, protesting about war, racism, or injustice. As they grew older, such causes gave way to the realities of making ends meet and providing for their families. They don't feel like protesting—they are comfortable in what they have already fought for and achieved. Therefore, parents are not very enthusiastic about the activism of teens.

There was a very funny line in a movie years ago that basically said, "They went in as revolutionaries and came out with government jobs." Protesting and activism, as one gets older, often becomes tempered by the settling effects of maturing.

The older you get the less turmoil you want in your life. Parents often want a predictable life, a routine schedule, and as

Key Note:

_____

_____

_____

_____

simple a life as possible. That is one reason the term that is often used to growing older is "settling down." No doubt you've heard people say, "He got married, had some kids, and 'settled down.'"

5. Parents are protective.

Parents want to make sure their children don't get hurt or feel pain. They remember the mistakes they made in their youth, and they try to prevent their children from making the same mistakes. Again, that is a sometimes positive approach, but it can become negative when parents become overprotective.

Protection is, however, a fact of parental life. No matter how long we exist as human beings, parents will always tend to be protective or even overprotective. As I have grown older and became a parent myself, I now realize the protection aspect of parenting much more fully. Whenever my children leave the house, I want to know where they are going, and I want to know that they are going to a supervised or wholesome environment. Why? Because I don't want them to get hurt.

They may see this response as prying into their business, but I want to protect them. This is a natural instinct of every parent. I often say mothers are especially protective because they had to go into the delivery room, endure great pain and discomfort to deliver their children into this world. Therefore, they especially feel the need to be protective. After being in the delivery room for the birth of my son and daughter, to this day I still do not understand how a woman can have more than one child. After seeing the pain that accompanied that experience, if I were a mother, my next child would be adopted!

6. Today's parents are busy.

Today's parents live at a pace that is unparalleled in the history of the human race. There is so much to do, but there never seems to be enough time in which to do it. Parents sometimes have two jobs, work late, or are involved in something that prevents them from being available for you. Often parents spend more time at work and on the road than they do at home. When dealing with the immediate issues of earning a living and of self-preservation, sometimes you seem to be an afterthought. Please understand your parents' hectic pace and that they are often very busy—providing a good life for you. It would be nice if it was not that way, but that is how the world turns today. This is especially the case in homes where there is only one parent. It is unfortunate but true that parents do not have the time they once had to care for children the way they should.

Remember, Teens

Parents are:
> Wise
> Settled
> Busy
> Practical
> Protective
> Realistic

Therefore, it is important for you to remember that:

1. If you honor your parents, God will honor you.
2. Parents are not always right, but they are in charge, and unless they grossly violate the rules of the game, you have no right to overturn or rebel against their decisions.
3. You need to pray for your parents.
4. You should earn responsibility.
5. Parents love and care for you unconditionally.

Key Note:

_____

_____

_____

_____

Chapter 10

A CHANGING WORLD, A CHANGING FAMILY

BY DAVID BURROWS

Are we distorted?
We kill a baby and say it's a fetus we aborted?
We dress two men up in a formal
Pronounce them married and call it normal.
Are we distorted?

Living in a Changing World

The world we live in has undergone significant changes in recent times. There has been drastic changes involving all aspects of society—many are not good.

For example, the family is in a state of decline and confusion, and it is being challenged in so many ways, both from within and without. Divorce has wreaked havoc in the lives of many young children and this often affects their development for years afterward. With the rise of divorce we have many un-parented or

Key Note:

_____

_____

_____

_____

under-parented children who have to find their way in life by themselves, because their families are in upheaval.

How can it be possible for a child to be stable if he or she lives in an unstable environment? It must be terribly confusing and upsetting for a child to spend one week with one parent and the next week with the other parent. Why is it so confusing for them? Because each parent gives them different rules, different environments, and different methods of discipline.

How can this kind of situation produce stability in a child's life? One parent may be very liberal and may allow a teen or pre-teen to drink alcohol and provide few limitations, but the other parent may be more strict. Which rules for living will that teenager adopt? In all likelihood, he or she will become confused and will not know which path to choose. This condition applies to a growing segment of the population worldwide.

Many of these unstable and confused teens get their "training" in the form of advice from rap artists and other entertainers. Imagine the impact on youth hearing the following lyrics (I have deleted the profanity):

This is the f....ing, sh..., I be talkin' bout,
Half rappin' ass mothafu....ers, you think it's a game?
You think it's a fu...in' game?....
Runnin' around here like some brand-new pus..y that's about to get fu...ed!"[1]

This is just one tragic example of the thousands of negative songs many children and teens listen to every day in their parents' house, in their parents' car, and on the home television set. This type of brain warping is influencing our children today.

Yes, the family is indeed changing, but not for the better. Unfortunately, divorce rates are not decreasing. There is a great lack of moral standards, positive values, and good role-modeling and the void is being filled with neglect and exposure to negative media. Regrettably, this situation is only likely to get worse. For example, when a girl becomes pregnant these days, a frequent question she may hear is, "Whose baby is it?" When people change their sex partners so often, this, sadly, becomes a legitimate question.

Alternative "Families"

There are a growing number of homosexuals and others with abnormal lifestyles and behaviors, who insist on creating "alternative families," which leave many young people wondering what a family really is. I believe this is a deplorable and unfortunate situation, especially when children are involved.

There are "families" that have two men or two women as parents of a child. The Bible simply doesn't accept such arrangements as families. A man and woman who marry and have children become a father and a mother—this is the family God spoke of throughout the Bible, the family structure that is complete and wholesome. I believe that any other arrangement is abnormal. When I use the term "abnormal," I am referring to family situations that differ from the original model.

Having two "mothers" or two "fathers" is an unnatural environment in which to raise children. Regardless of how inappropriate and improper these situations are to me, many of our social scientists, doctors, and even some pastors and religious leaders are attempting to pronounce such arrangements as "normal." I believe this is a distorted point of view.

Many argue that homosexuals are born that way, but if this were true, it would mean that these people are born with an

Key Note:

_____

_____

_____

_____

abnormal attraction. You cannot have two definitions of normal. If you believe a man who is attracted to a female is normal, then it would have to be abnormal for a male to be attracted to a male, or a female to be attracted to a female. In this case I would have to say that the homosexual's signals have to be crossed. I personally cannot believe that anyone is truly born as a homosexual—it would mean a birth of mixed signals because males are attracted to females by nature. Are some people born unnatural? Does God create people that way? I don't believe so.

The definition of traditional marriage is being challenged politically and socially as never before, and, in many cases, traditional marriage is being replaced by same-sex variations that are sure to add to the confusion being experienced by today's youth.

The young person today asks, "Which one of these arrangements is a true marriage?" And many must be asking, "Exactly what is marriage?"

Gang "Families"

Another alternative family style that has risen out of the ashes caused by the demise of the traditional family is the gang. For many years I worked with gang members and the stories I heard from them are truly unbelievable. As a result, I've concluded that the formation of gangs is not accidental; rather, it is a direct result of neglect and abuse.

Take BJ, for example. He was abandoned by his parents at age 13 and has had to live on his own, getting money, love, and whatever other needs he has by whatever means possible. The only "family" he knew was the gang that accepted him.

Another young man I worked with had a mother who was a cocaine addict and a father who disowned him at birth. He, too, ended up with his "family" being the neighborhood gang.

Can we really expect anything positive from our young people when they grow up in these types of environments?

Another young man I worked with did not know who his father was until he became a young adult, and when he did locate his father, he found him in jail! He went to prison to visit his father, and he asked his father why he never tried to find him or have a relationship with him. The father could not give a real or satisfying answer to his son. Before leaving, the son asked if they could get together when the father was released from prison. The man replied, "I can't make no promises."

What Happened to the Traditional Family?

What is a parent? What is a family? There was a time when these questions were easily answered, but as we look around, we see that times have changed. Public schools give answers that greatly differ from the concepts of family living that previous generations understood without difficulty. There was a time when the only kind of parents that existed was a father and mother who were married and had children—a couple who carried the same name and characteristics of their parents. But today, it is hard to define what a typical family really is.

Many young people cannot identify with the illustrations in the Bible that deal with a father and a son. They don't quite understand what it means to have a real father to whom they can relate. That is why it is so wrong to have children outside of a traditional family structure. All too often, children have to grow up either sharing a father or having no father or mother influence at all. Sometimes this means that they must become their own

Key Note:

_____

_____

_____

_____

parent even before they become an adult. Society today is full of one-parent homes, and some of those homes have a parent who is there in name only. Children and society pay a high price for this situation, but it is the children who suffer the most.

There is quite a bit of teaching in churches and society about being good husbands and wives, but rarely do we hear teachings about parents and children, particularly teenagers. This problem is so significant that society has coined terms such as, "Generation X" to identify a group of young adults. As a result, many teens have problems relating to their parents, and many parents have major problems relating to their teens. Some parents can't seem to cope with the responsibilities of parenting at all, and some teens can't cope with their pressures either. What can be done to change this situation? The purpose of this book is to answer those very questions.

"Where Are You, Adam?"

It is interesting to note that the first recorded marriage in the Bible ends up with God asking an intriguing question. He asks, "Adam, where are you?" (See Genesis 3:9.) Of course God knew where Adam was, but I believe He was asking the question for Adam's (man's) sake. In effect, God was saying, "Mr. Head of the house, where are you? Are you in the position you should be? What happened to your family?" That question remains as relevant today as it was in the Garden. God and the world await the answer to this question, "Man, mister, father, where are you?"

All too often the correct answer would be, "I am MIA" or "I'm AWOL." Unfortunately, many fathers today are missing in action or absent without leave. When the man is supposed to be in the home, he is frequently out playing some kind of game, or involved in something other than his family life. When he is supposed to be caring for his family, he is often somewhere he shouldn't be and sometimes he's there with a woman other than his wife, the one he made a solemn commitment to.

In many societies today a disturbing phenomenon is taking place. Women are excelling, going to school, striving for achievement, and becoming breadwinners, while the men are spending their lives in a bar, on the corner, in the club, or in prison! In most Western countries, especially among non-white populations, at least 90 percent of the inmates in penal institutions are male. The question needs to be raised again, as God did in the Book of Genesis, "Adam (Man), where are you?"

What Happened to Daddy and Mommy?

There was a time when children learned about life from their parents. Mommy was the role model for little Susie, and daddy was the role model for little Johnny. Mommy would take Susie under her care and teach her how to be a lady. As a result, Susie would learn how to cook, sew, and take care of certain things around the house as a result of watching mommy do these things. She would learn how to dress and fix her hair, and when it was time, mommy would sit down with Susie and tell her about "the birds and the bees"—the "facts of life."

Meanwhile, daddy would show little Johnny how to be a man. He would play ball with him and strive to be his son's hero. As a result, Johnny would say, "I want to be like you, dad. You know I want to be like you." Little boys used to be proud of their

Key Note:

_____

_____

_____

_____

fathers, and daddy would point little Johnny in the right direction. Oh, how times have changed!

What often happens today is that daddy leaves home when the child is young or he isn't there to begin with. He simply provides the sperm necessary to make a baby. Many men have children here and around the corner, and sometimes their progeny can be found in the next state or the next country! He may telephone his kids once in a while or even visit them, but it's not enough, for little Johnny doesn't care anymore. He thinks daddy is worthless—a no-good bum, and sometimes he even grows up to hate his dad! The sad reality is that he will end up repeating the process with his own children. Therefore, the process of disappointment and hurt followed by anger and disillusionment will breed resentment and hate in succeeding generations.

After growing up without a father or having a part-time father, many young men don't even care if they have a relationship with daddy or not. The boy has already gone through the pain of not having a father and now he is too bitter to care. Consequently, he identifies with his friends, who unfortunately will many times grow up only to repeat the same process, while expressing their anger in violent and destructive ways. I know many young men in my neighborhood who were the sons of absent, alcoholic, or abusive fathers. They grew up hating their fathers and swearing not to be like them, only to repeat the same behaviors when they grew up!

In the majority of homes in North America and the Caribbean today the only parent is a mother. She sometimes works two jobs just so she and the children can survive. She ends up being a role model for both sexes not by choice, but by default. Isn't it interesting to note how many athletes greet viewers, as they are being interviewed on television, not by saying "Hi, dad," but by saying, "Hi, mom"? This is a very revealing phenomenon that reflects what is happening in many homes today

Unfortunately, many mothers today do not have time to teach their children the things they need to know. Some believe it is more important to have a comfortable lifestyle that they place the children in front of the television, or turn them over to a babysitter and go off to work.

Another increasing and alarming problem is when a father abandons his children and the mother's new boyfriend moves in, which sometimes results in the new "father figure" molesting young daughters. The girls don't report these men because they believe their mothers will get angry and no one will believe them.

When Paul wrote, "*Children, obey your parents*" (Eph. 6:1), he was obviously telling children to obey their fathers and mothers. Today fathers and mothers living together as the parents in a home sometimes represent only 30 to 40 percent of the population in many areas!

If Paul were writing his letter to the Ephesians today, he would have to say, "Children, obey your parents, your guardians, your stepparents, your two mommies, your two daddies, a man who lives in the house, or your grandmother." Today's family is not the traditional family of just a few generations ago. Soon some people may be petitioning to marry their dog or cat. Don't laugh too loudly, this is not so farfetched as you may think. Unfortunately, whether we like it or not, the family has changed and it continues to change. Today's child is learning to deal with

Key Note:

_____

_____

_____

_____

one-parent families, step-families, absentee parents, parents who visit, and parents who occasionally send their regards.

In addition to what has been previously mentioned, there are many blended families—families usually formed after divorces and remarriages. The difficulty: children in these families have multiple parents with multiple influences, and they have to adjust to new siblings, as well. This creates authority and discipline problems. Sometimes the parents in these families fight each other and use their children as pawns.

Role Reversals and Role Confusion

Another interesting shift in today's family involves role reversals and role confusion. We now have female "super-heroes" who fight men. We have men who want to have babies and wear dresses. And there are other examples of role reversals and confusion.

It is very obvious to me that it was not God's intention to have a woman fighting for a living or engaged in any kind of fighting whatsoever. Men were built by their Manufacturer for certain distinct purposes, and women were created for other purposes. Men do not have breasts with milk; therefore, sucking a man's breast is an abuse of what God intended. A woman was designed with certain curves on her body to give her grace, beauty, and attractiveness. Instead of such shapely curves, a man has bumps, bulges, and sometimes rounded bellies!

I believe that two parents, in their proper roles as male and female role models (father and mother), is the best environment for raising healthy and happy children and a stable society. Unfortunately, the original concept of the family seems to be dying a slow and painful death for a multitude of reasons including divorce, pornography, abuse, and the "original sin."

So what can do we do about the changing family?

Endnote

1. Artist DMX. album, "And Then There Was X"; song, "What's My Name."

Key Note:

_____

_____

_____

_____

PART III

Connecting Principles

By David Burrows

Chapter 11

RELATING TO TEENS

By David Burrows

Earning Respect

*H*ow *do parents* earn the respect of their children and retain the rights inherent in their position?

1. Parents should provide for their children.

It is the responsibility of parents to provide for their children. Children do not ask to be born. Whenever children are brought into this world, the parent or parents have the responsibility of providing all the necessities for their children, according to the parents' abilities to do so. Note what the Bible says concerning this responsibility:

> *...After all, children should not have to save up for their parents, but parents for their children* (2 Corinthians 12:14 NIV).

Parents should provide food, shelter, and clothing for their children in line with their ability to do so. Parents should not

> **Key Note:**
>
> _____
>
> _____
>
> _____
>
> _____

waste money by buying everything their children desire, however. Many times children lack discretion; as a result, they would buy anything they could. After all, they don't have to work. You should not have children if you are not prepared to provide for them.

2. Parents should not provoke their children.

Parents should not abuse the authority God gave to them by abusing their children, by failing to provide for them, or by living a life of double standards. "Provoking children" could mean being too restrictive, abusive, or unfair with regard to expectations or living contrary to God's Word and still expecting children to obey without question. Note again what the Bible says:

Fathers, do not exasperate your children; instead, bring them up in the training and instruction of the Lord (Ephesians 6:4 NIV).

Parents should remember that their teens are only a few years away from becoming parents themselves. The teenagers of today will become the parents of tomorrow. Today's parents must ensure that their way of life does not drive their children in the wrong direction. Rather, their lifestyle should point young people toward the path they want them to follow.

3. Parents should care for their children.

Scripture states, "...*Children are a reward from Him*" (Ps. 127:3 NIV). However, in today's busy and mixed-up society, children are very frequently seen more as a burden than as a treasure. Parents sometimes don't care about or for their children. Caring does not mean simply providing for their children's daily needs; it also means teaching them the difference between right and wrong and taking time to see that their concerns are taken care of and their questions about life are answered.

A parent who cares will spend time with his or her children and talk to them about what the children want to talk about. Many teens become distant from their parents because of their parents' one-way communication with them. Some parents only talk to their children when the children are in trouble or when they failed to carry out an assigned task.

Your conversations with your teen should not only consist of: "Have you mowed the lawn like I asked you to?"; "Did you do the dishes as you were instructed?"; "Did you clean your room"? It is also important to talk to your children about things they want to discuss. Ask teens about their favorite music group or their favorite basketball team or player. Ask them about school, their friends, and their plans for the future. The more you talk with them, the more you learn about them. Parents must take good care of what God has entrusted to them.

4. Parents are supposed to discipline their children.

The issue of discipline is a big one for both parents and teens. Teenagers know that discipline is a painful part of love, and they actually want to be disciplined. A parent who takes time to correct a young person may not be liked at the moment when the discipline is administered, but he or she will be respected. The Bible states very clearly that if you ignore discipline, your children will go astray. How many times have you seen a spoiled brat? Worse yet, a rich spoiled brat? No one likes to be around that type of child—discipline gives your children an advantage beyond monetary.

Of course, when a child reaches those teen years, the methods of discipline employed by the parents should change.

Key Note:

_____

_____

_____

_____

Younger children often need physical discipline. However, if a child has been under your care for 13 years and does not respond to your discipline, you must not have disciplined properly during the earlier years. In such a case physical punishment is no longer the answer. The revocation of privileges, added chores, stricter curfews, restrictions as to where they can go, or reduced allowances can be used to discipline a teen. Keep in mind that the discipline needs to be appropriate for the given situation.

In administering discipline, however, parents should not enforce what has not been defined. Parents should communicate very clearly to teens what the ground rules, expectations, and boundaries are and what the consequences will be for crossing those boundaries. If the teen violates a rule that was already clearly defined and agreed upon, the only thing left to do is accept the punishment.

5. Parents must encourage their children.

Encouragement is a part of nurturing. Parents must be there for their children. You, as a parent, might take it lightly when you don't keep a promise, but your teens won't. Let your word be good. Show up for the play in which they are performing. Be at the ball game when they play. If they make good grades, reward them. Even if they make mistakes, encourage them to try again and to do better.

If you have good children, don't frustrate them. I have seen parents whose children are well-behaved, ordinary kids, yet they treat them as if they were the most rotten teens in the world. Thank God if you have teens who keep their word, don't do drugs, and are not promiscuous. Give them more responsibility as they demonstrate the ability to be trusted. I have also known of parents who denied their children attendance at a church or youth group meeting as a punishment. Don't do that. Youth groups and church are the two places where they are most likely to get discipline and good counsel. Youths need responsibility in order to grow.

6. Parents need to listen and try to relate.

Another old saying that relates to young people is: "Children should be seen and not heard." That is simply wrong. Children need a forum in which to be heard. If you don't provide them with a forum where they can be heard, there are many people who will, and those people don't have your heart, and they don't really care about your children. Parents must understand what motivates their children, what interests them, what music they listen to, which books they read, and who they consider to be their heroes.

Parents who don't know what music their children listen to are out of touch. Today's musicians and entertainers tell teens to get high, kill, steal, rape, and rebel. Stop by your nearest music store and read the lyrics to popular songs. Or check out the lyrics of the songs on the Internet.

If you know what music your children listen to, you have a better idea of where their heads are. You won't be able to become a teenager again, but you must learn how to relate to your teenager. Ask your teens questions such as, "What are some of the new sayings among teens today? What do they mean?" Often theirs is a far different world from ours, a world to which parents don't have ready access. Parents must listen and relate to their teenagers, or they will lose touch with them and just call

Key Note:

_____

_____

_____

_____

it a "generation gap." A parent's world is obvious to teens, but a teen's world is not obvious to parents. Parents may assume a lot and yet know very little.

7. Parents must communicate.

There is no excuse for not communicating with your teenagers, and here I mean two-way communication. Every parent-teen relationship needs a forum in which conflicts may be resolved. Also, parents should learn to say, "We're sorry" when they are wrong and to forgive when necessary. Forgiveness gets rid of bitterness.

Parents must also remember to keep problems at home or between themselves and a counselor. Parents' friends do not need to know what is happening between the parents and their children. Young people do not want to hear about how their parents talk about them to other parents. When they do so, they will, in all probability, communicate with their parents even less than before.

Parents must take the idealism of youth and help it merge with realism. Youths ask many questions, and parents need to help them find the answers. Parents don't need to tell teens not to ask the questions. Punishment is not an appropriate way for parents to escape their parental responsibility of face-to-face communication.

8. Parents must prepare teenagers for the future.

Believe it or not, children are only supposed to be with their parents for a period of time. Children are born to leave home. A parent's job is to prepare their children to leave home. The best parents are the ones whose children are well-prepared to live outside the confines of their home.

As teens grow, they should progressively be given more responsibility and encouraged to start their own lives by planning for the future. The worst thing for a young person who is "mommy's boy" or "daddy's girl" is to get married and expect to have the same experiences as in the parents' home. When that doesn't happen, the young person may run back home to daddy or mommy. Parents should not smother young people or prepare them to stay in their house forever. Parents need to learn to commit their children to God.

After parents have done what they should and could, there is nothing left for them to do. Parents must exercise wisdom, but remember to let the children go after you have done your best and keep praying for them.

Parents must remember that approximately 80 percent of teen learning comes from visual observations. Teens often don't listen to what we say, but you can be sure that they are watching our lives!

Key Note:

_____

_____

_____

_____

Chapter 12

RELATING TO PARENTS

BY DAVID BURROWS

Teens: This chapter is for you. It gives you ways that you can most effectively relate to and get along with your parents.

God's original plan for the family was one man, one woman, and their children. (See Genesis 2:24.) The man was responsible under God to take care of his wife and children. The woman was responsible to be her husband's partner and helper. Both were responsible for teaching their children and providing love, discipline, and respect for them. The Bible has specific guidelines about how the family is supposed to relate to each other.

For this reason a man will leave his father and mother... (Ephesians 5:31 NIV).

Children, obey your parents in the Lord, for this is right. 'Honor your father and mother'—which is the first commandment with a promise—'that it may go well with you and that you may enjoy long life on the earth.' Fathers, do not exasperate your

Key Note:

_____

_____

_____

_____

children; instead, bring them up in the training and instruction of the Lord (Ephesians 6:1-4 NIV).

So, as you can see, the original plan was very simple, indeed. A man and his wife would live together, love each other, and bring up children together. They were to pass on to their children the instructions God had given to them. This plan was interrupted, however, by the Fall of man, his disobedience to and defiance of God's clear instructions. As a result, mankind became separated from God; therefore, the family was also disconnected from God. Man forgot, or no longer understood, the purpose God had for the family. When God's purpose is not known or understood, abuse is inevitable.

Man abused the very thing God had designed for his protection, that which would give him the stability he needs in order to survive. These tragic errors have brought drastic consequences to the human race. The destruction of humanity and God's plan continues to take place.

Can you imagine growing up in a home where two women live together as a man and woman should? God's original plan can hardly be recognized in today's world. In the Book of Genesis, not too long after the first family was created, God could no longer confidently deal with any family unit. The Bible says He had to search for a man who would teach his children.

For I have chosen him, so that he will direct his children and his household after him to keep the way of the Lord by doing what is right and just, so that the Lord will bring about for Abraham what he has promised him (Genesis 18:19 NIV).

God had to search for a man who would teach his family. Does that remind you of anything? God thinks it is important for families to work in unity, according to His original plan. If even one link is missing, there is potential for chaos.

What's a Teen to Do?

1. Teens need to obey their parents "*in the Lord.*"

Parents outrank children. Parents have a higher position in the family unit. According to God's law, teens must recognize their parents' position and respect it. Your parents are not always right, but they are in charge, and unless they grossly violate the rules of the game, you have no right to overturn or rebel against their decisions.

There should be discussion in your family. Your point of view should be known, but the final say belongs to your parents, the "generals" who were commissioned by the Commander-in-Chief. The Scripture following shows how God feels about parental instruction:

> *Listen, my son [and daughter], to your father's instruction and do not forsake your mother's teaching. They will be a garland to grace your head and a chain to adorn your neck* (Prov. 1:8-9 NIV).

Listen to your parents' instruction unless it is obviously out of line with God's Word. You cannot really be expected to obey a parent who asks you to take drugs or rob a bank, but you are expected to obey a parent who gives you reasonable instructions in a spirit of love and fairness. Pray for your parents and do your best to help them understand your point of view, but unless they blatantly go against God, you should always obey them.

Key Note:

_____

_____

_____

_____

2. Teens must respect their parents.

The Bible issues a very clear command that has a blessing attached to it. The command is to honor your father and mother:

> *"Honor your father and mother"—which is the first commandment with a promise—"that it may go well with you and that you may enjoy long life on the earth"* (Ephesians 6:2-3 NIV).

In other words, respect your parents. They are your caretakers in this world until you are old enough and wise enough to make it on your own. Until that time, and even after you leave home, you should always respect and honor your parents. It is important not to be disrespectful or ashamed of your parents. This is the one command from God that indicates He is not pleased when you are disrespectful to your parents. In fact, this command indicates that your life may be shortened if you fail to respect your parents. If you dishonor your parents, God will dishonor you. He said so very clearly.

3. Teens deserve responsibility.

Don't ask for more responsibility until you act correctly with what you already have. If your parents give you a curfew and you agree to be home at 11 P.M., and you come home with a false story about a flat tire at 1 A.M., they should not even let you out of the house during daylight hours. So if you want more responsibility, live up to your part of the bargain. You should keep your word so well that they can't help but see how responsible you are and increase the amount of freedom you have. If you know you will be late for a legitimate reason, make sure you call them and let them know. Don't make your parents worry because of the dumb things. Parents are proud of responsible children. If you are supposed to go to school party, don't sneak off with a friend and lie about it. The more you cheat and lie, the less responsibility you will deserve. If you choose not to be responsible, your parents are supposed to discipline you. This Scripture from the

Book of Proverbs shows the role discipline plays in the mind of the Lord:

> *My son, do not despise the Lord's discipline and do not resent his rebuke, because the Lord disciplines those He loves, as a father the son he delights in* (Proverbs 3:11-12 NIV).

Good parents discipline in love because they want their children to be responsible. If you are irresponsible, your parents will have to discipline you.

4. Teens need to pray for their parents.

Parents should listen to and understand teens, but it is one of the realities of life today that they often don't. Many times when I talk to teens they say, "Talk to my parents? Are you kidding? I have tried and tried but they won't listen to me or appreciate my point of view." Because that is so often true, you may have to appeal to the Commander-in-Chief and say, "Chief, you are in charge of this situation. Help my parents understand and communicate with me."

You may be surprised at what good can be done and what can be accomplished if you pray regularly for your parents. Your parents are not your enemies. You can do all you know to do and talk to your parents, but if your parent is obnoxious and unwilling to cooperate, you can only pray and continue to do your best despite the circumstances. Be as helpful and as cooperative as possible, and don't be the one to cause further problems or aggravate the situation. Give your parents a reason to appreciate

Key Note:

_____

_____

_____

_____

you and understand you better. Show them that you know how to love. Let them see truth, honesty, and love in your life.

5. Teens should report a parent who is grossly out of order.

If your parents abuse you physically or sexually, you are no longer obligated to obey them "in the Lord." Perhaps for your own physical and mental survival you need to report your parents to the appropriate authorities and get out of the situation until some resolution can be made. Sometimes things happen in step-parent or other non-traditional family units that result in a need for you to get out of a situation quickly. In fact, problems can develop even in normal or traditional family units that require you take action for your own protection. But before you do so, consult your youth pastor, guidance counselor, or another adult in whom you have confidence.

All authorities and power are ultimately subject to God. If parents are grossly violating God's law, there are some people with appropriate "authority" who can and will deal with them. The Book of Romans speaks very clearly about this topic. The following verses show that parents, teens, citizens, and governments are all responsible to a higher authority.

> *Everyone must submit himself to the governing authorities, for there is no authority except that which God has established. The authorities that exist have been established by God. Consequently, he who rebels against the authority is rebelling against what God has instituted, and those who do so will bring judgment on themselves. For rulers hold no terror for those who do right, but for those who do wrong. Do you want to be free from fear of the one in authority? Then do what is right and he will commend you. For he is God's servant to do you good. But if you do wrong, be afraid, for he does not bear the sword for nothing...* (Romans 13:1-4 NIV).

6. Some teens have no parents.

In today's world, some children actually have to grow up on their own. In fact, many children the world over are growing up on their own or at least partly on their own. A parent may be there, but may not provide or fulfill any of the appropriate parental functions. Some teens have to "grow themselves up" and look to others who are not their parents for direction, guidance, and counsel. If this is the case with you, it is important to talk to someone and to be able to get help when you need it or to get advice in making decisions. In some cases you could talk to a school counselor, a youth pastor, a pastor, a Christian friend, or an adult in whom you have confidence.

Some young people have to be their own parent and in some cases must be a parent to their own parents. Many times, through your godly living and example, you will be able to teach your parents how to live and how to be responsible. God will help you as you continue to serve Him and place Him first in your life. No matter how difficult the situation is, "hold fast" to the things you have learned in the Word and let God do the rest.

Key Note:

_____

_____

_____

_____

Chapter 13

PRACTICAL WISDOM TIPS FOR PARENTS

By David Burrows

The following life-saving tips have been acquired from serving many years as a youth pastor and a parent of teens. This practical wisdom has been proven effective time and time again.

TELEVISION. Remove TVs from children's bedrooms and place it/them only in a "public" viewing area. While there is no guarantee that this will stop teens from viewing offensive material, it does serve as a deterrent, especially during late night hours. I have found that grades improve and the risk of addictions to inappropriate material is diminished when teens cannot lock their doors and spend unsupervised hours watching television.

THE INTERNET. Take the same steps with computers and the internet as I've outlined about TVs. Pornography is quite possibly the number one item on the internet. Pornographers are aggressive and really don't care about the age, status, or religious beliefs of their viewers. They go after both young people and older people. By making sure that computers are only in a

Key Note:

_____

_____

_____

_____

public area of the home (the family room, office, living room, or kitchen), you, as a parent, are better able to monitor what is happening on the computer. This makes it more difficult for a teen to get caught up in unwanted internet activity.

There are many other dangers on the internet, as well. For example, there are pedophiles who recruit children and young people via internet chat rooms by posing as children themselves, and there are even suicide sites that exploit vulnerable teens by encouraging them to commit suicide. Likewise, there are various groups, such as white supremacist organizations, terrorists of various sorts, and many other social deviants who use the internet for their nefarious purposes.

Monitor your teen's involvement with the internet at all times. Filtering software is available that filters out certain types of material on your computer. It would be important to talk to a computer provider to discuss what would be the best ways to establish the appropriate security measures on your computer to prevent offensive material from being displayed to anyone, especially your teens. Computer systems have the ability to set parameters at different levels in order to prevent material you don't want to be downloaded. It is also important to check the internet viewing history on your computer to make sure that unhealthy sites are not being visited. Most computer stores are able to advise you concerning the steps you should take to get the desired protection and security you want for your teens.

STEP-PARENTS. In a situation where there are stepparents or blended families, it is important for the natural parent to be the one who speaks to his or her son or daughter about discipline, primarily because young people often use the retort that the other parent is not "my real parent". Young people often use this to create division and confusion in the home and family. Of course you don't want to add to or reinforce that kind of division, so it is important for both parents to be in agreement, but if there is an issue that needs to be addressed, the natural parent ought to be the one who talks to the child about it.

FAMILY DEVOTIONS. Devotions are another key for maintaining family unity, and this time also provides a great opportunity for families to be together. I believe there is great truth in the saying, "The family that prays together stays together." Having devotions is certainly not a guarantee of success, but it definitely increases a family's chances for establishing and maintaining healthy relationships. As we get our priorities right, particularly with regard to spiritual things, families will thrive. I believe there is no greater priority than to fulfill the greatest command that was given to mankind: to love, reverence, and respect God. When this principle is instilled in children, it prevents them from falling into the many traps set by the evil one. Children who see that their parents have a healthy respect and reverence for God will more than likely carry that same respect with them into their adult lives, even if they stray away at times.

FAMILY MEETINGS. Another underestimated but highly effective tool for families is the regular family meeting. This is a time that is set aside for parents and teens to make decisions, find out what is going on in each other's lives, and to disseminate information or discipline. This format is effective because it allows children and teens to have a say within the family process. My wife and I have had family meetings with our teens, and during these times we found out what was going on in their school, social, and spiritual lives. Sometimes our teens

Key Note:

_____

_____

_____

_____

were surprisingly open, while at other times the meeting format allowed for easy two-way communication to be initiated. We also used these times to plan vacations together, ask for their opinions on critical issues, or simply had fun learning about each other. We would often ask for an informal report from our daughter and son about what was happening at school, in the neighborhood, or in church youth programs. We also used the opportunity to give them guidance with their choices of friends, places to go, and things to do.

VACATION. One of the greatest traditions in our family was the annual family vacation. Although families live in the same house, because of busy schedules for both parents and teens today, they may not actually spend much time together. It's unfortunate to see how stressful the lives of some teenagers have become. I remember remarking to my son one day that he had more appointments and meetings than I had! Vacation is a time of respite and release for us—a wonderful family time for bonding, fun, relaxation, and a great break from the wear and tear of everyday life. Even God took a "vacation", so why shouldn't we? No matter what your budget is, be sure to take some time as a family to get away from your everyday (sometimes stressful) environment and enjoy the scenery of another area or culture.

KEEPING THEM CLOSE. One of the keys to whatever success I have had with my teens was by keeping them close to me. By keeping them close I mean physically close. Don't leave them with others or at home when you can take them along to the store or the market. The time you spend with your teen is an investment that will pay off abundantly in the future. From the time my son could walk, he would go wherever I went. We would go together to basketball games, softball games, my work, and to church—in short, wherever I went, he went. The same was true with my daughter. As they got older, during the phase when teens normally don't want to be around their parents, my children still were delighted to be with me. Of course my work as a youth pastor meant that they got to do fun things at church, but they seemed to find it easy to be with me no matter where we were.

FUN AND PLAY. Parents and fun are not words that are usually synonymous. However, sometimes a family needs to play together. Make time to have some form of play to enjoy together. We would swim in the pool, play ball together, make jokes, or play games such as Scrabble, dominoes, or cards. These were fun things that brought our family together. After all, being able to play and have fun releases some of the stress in your life, and it allows your mind to get away from everyday issues.

ASK QUESTIONS. Asking questions is the only way to know what is happening in your teen's life. So, be sure to ask questions, especially if you notice any changes, either good or bad, in your teen's life. There usually are behind-the-scenes reasons for changes in behavior, attitude, and associations. Don't wait until these changes have taken permanent effect in your teen's life to begin asking questions—then it may be too late to help. A strategically asked question can help you gain information, whether your teen's response is frank and open or evasive. If the answer is frank, then you have skipped the drama of having to dig further. If the answer is evasive, you may need to ask additional questions to get the truth and prevent a disaster. Ask what they do, who they associate with, and why they do certain things. This shows them that you care. The question, "Why?" is one of the most important questions you can ever ask. For example, you

Key Note:

_____

_____

_____

_____

may want to ask, "Why do you want to go to this party; who is going to be there?"

BEHAVIOR VS. NATURE. One mistake that parents often make is to call a child or teen by a term related to their behavior. When teenagers do something dumb, don't call them "dumb" or "stupid," or any such epithet. We need to separate the person from the behavior. Because a child does something stupid does not mean she is a fool. It simply means she has engaged in stupid behavior, just like all of us have done from time to time, especially when we were young. Instead of labeling a teen as stupid, just say, "That was a dumb thing you did," and work on helping him to change that behavior instead of labeling him for life. Anyone's behavior can be modified through discipline and incentives. Always be sure to separate the behavior from the person.

Some kids just seem to be sloppy by nature, and some are naturally neat. Have them put things in their place so as to help them modify any sloppiness or disorganized behavior in their lives. In the early years, spanking is the most effective tool parents have to reinforce and alter their child's behavior. In later years, other things may work better. For example, grounding is an option that many parents use. One thing that has worked very effectively for me is fines. I adopted this procedure from the NBA and NFL. When players become violent, the NBA and NFL levy monetary fines upon them for fighting. Once this system was instituted, the incidences of violence and fighting in the leagues were reduced. Nothing gets the attention of people more quickly than taking away their money. When I would tell my children to do certain things and they didn't follow through, I would have a meeting with them and tell them, "If you fail to do this or pick up that, or if your room is not clean, you will be fined $10 per incident." This approach quickly got their attention. It might not work for everyone, but you can think of other creative ways to help your teenager make adjustments in behavior.

CREATIVE DISCIPLINE. In some countries there are laws that basically take away the rights of parents to physically discipline their children. We all know that abuse occurs, and there clearly is a need to protect children from abusive parents. There are many parents, however, who are not abusive and who clearly understand the importance of physical discipline. Many of these parents believe in the Bible-based adage: "Spare the rod and spoil the child." Because of society's laws, these parents may feel they are forced to allow their children to throw tantrums, and they can only issue warnings and threats. When this happens, the children soon recognize that the warnings and threats have no "teeth," because their parents do not follow up on them. While I do not support abuse, I am fully in agreement that loving, educated parents can apply physical discipline in certain circumstances. Of course, I believe that this type of discipline was designed for the early years when the understanding of children is limited. As a child gets older, there should be less need for physical discipline, because the child has already been trained physically with regard to right and wrong behavior.

One creative discovery for me came from a well-known family counselor and psychologist, who noted that there is a muscle located in the neck and shoulder region called the trapezius muscle. Squeezing this muscle causes no permanent damage, yet it reinforces the physical message you want to send. I used "the squeeze" effectively for many years to the point where all I had to do was hold up my index finder and thumb and my children

Key Note:

_____

_____

_____

_____

knew it was time to adjust their behavior or face "the squeeze." Another creative avenue was the use of a handshake. When my son would do something wrong and was not getting the message, I would simply give him a handshake and squeeze his hand so hard that he would get the message. It is important to find creative means of discipline and to be faithful in using what you find to be effective for you. I believe that the government is often comprised of people who are not godly or effective parents, and have no moral authority to tell us how to discipline our children. Who decided that the Bible method of discipline was irrelevant?

LISTENING. Another very important concept in parenting is the art of listening. Most parents communicate with their children by talking to them, but not necessarily by listening to them. The older our children get, the more we must focus on two-way communication with them. Frequently, what we don't hear from our teens is a lot more important than what we do hear. As your children move through the teen years, they may tend to try and lock you out of their world, and the only way to enter their world is by talking with them and listening to them. If you dismiss their concerns or don't give them a voice, someone else surely will.

BE ATTENTIVE. The final concept is the importance of being attentive to your children and teens. Be aware of what your kids are listening to, watching, and doing on the internet. Sometimes if you are attentive, you will stumble on life-and-death issues that you were not aware of. For example, a note might fall on the ground or a message could be left on a computer screen or a comment might be written in a yearbook that, if interpreted correctly, will lead to an understanding of what the young person is going through or planning. Many times parents miss clues that could have prevented a tragedy. As a case in point, the student perpetrators who were involved in the Columbine shooting incident worked on their computers in secret. They sent out messages that could have prevented the violence if someone had discovered them sooner. I am sure their parents did their best, but they may have missed important clues that could have changed the outcome. Always strive to be attentive!

Key Note:

_____

_____

_____

_____

Chapter 14

THE WORD ON PARENTS AND TEENS

By David Burrows

When I write, I provide insights from the Bible regarding the issues. Whether you are a Christian, Muslim, Jew, Hindu, or agnostic, it is clear that the words in the Bible provide valuable insights for successfully living. It is amazing to me how the Bible supplies the answers to so many of today's problems and so correctly describes how we should live and act to bring out our potential—adults and children. Because I believe the truths in the Bible, I include Scriptures relevant to my topic.

I list them so they will be easily available to you as a reference. Of particular interest to me are the writings of Solomon in the Books of Proverbs and Ecclesiastes—truly some of my favorite Bible passages. I have arranged them topically here so parents and teens can review them and use them as personal references to apply to their lives. I believe you will find these words to be very significant and life-changing, as I have.

Key Note:

_____

_____

_____

_____

The Word for Parents

Parents should be examples and not live by double standards: "*Fathers, do not exasperate your children; instead, bring them up in the training and instruction of the Lord*" (Eph. 6:4 NIV).

Parents are supposed to provide for children: "*But if any provide not for his own, and especially for those of his own house, he hath denied the faith, and is worse than an infidel*" (1 Tim. 5:8).

"*Now I am ready to visit you for the third time, and I will not be a burden to you, because what I want is not your possessions but you. After all, children should not have to save up for their parents, but parents for their children*" (2 Cor. 12:14 NIV).

Parents, don't forget that children are a heritage from the Lord. (See Psalm 127:3.)

The Word for Teens

Remember your Creator now: "*Remember your Creator in the days of your youth, before the days of trouble come and the years approach when you will say, 'I find no pleasure in them'— before the sun and the light and the moon and the stars grow dark, and the clouds return after the rain; when the keepers of the house tremble, and the strong men stoop, when the grinders cease because they are few, and those looking through the windows grow dim*" (Eccles. 12:1-3 NIV).

Obey your parents: "*Children, obey your parents in the Lord, for this is right*" (Eph. 6:1, NIV).

Honor your parents and preserve your life: "*Honor your father and mother*"—which is the first commandment with a promise—"*that it may go well with you and that you may enjoy long life on the earth*" (Eph. 6:2-3 NIV).

Respect authority and submit to it: "*Everyone must submit himself to the governing authorities, for there is no authority except that which God has established. The authorities that exist have been established by God. Consequently, he who rebels against the authority is rebelling against what God has instituted, and those who do so will bring judgment on themselves. For rulers hold no terror for those who do* *right, but for those who do wrong. Do you want to be free from fear of the one in authority? Then do what is right and he will commend you. For he is God's servant to do you good. But if you do wrong, be afraid, for he does not bear the sword for nothing. He is God's servant, an agent of wrath to bring punish mention the wrongdoer. Therefore, it is necessary to submit to the authorities, not only because of possible punishment but also because of conscience"* (Rom. 13:1-5 NIV).

Pray for authority so your life will be peaceful: *"I urge, then, first of all, that requests, prayers, intercession and thanksgiving be made for everyone—for kings and for all those in authority, that we may live peaceful and quiet lives in all godliness and holiness"* (1 Tim. 2:1-2 NIV).

Listen to your parents' instructions: *"Listen, my son, to your father's instruction and do not forsake your mother's teaching. They will be a garland to grace your head and a chain to adorn your neck"* (Prov. 1:8-9 NIV).

Avoid bad company: *"My son, if sinners entice you, do not give in to them. If they say, 'Come along with us; let's lie in wait for someone's blood, let's waylay some harmless soul; let's swallow them alive, like the grave, [Hebrew: Sheol] and whole, like those who go down to the pit; we will get all sorts of valuable things and fill our houses with plunder; throw in your lot with us, and we will share a common purse'—my son, do not go along with them, do not set foot on their paths; for their feet rush into sin, they are swift to shed blood. How useless to spread a net in full view of all the birds! These men lie in wait for their own blood; they*

Key Note:

_____

_____

_____

_____

waylay only themselves! Such is the end of all who go after ill-gotten gain; it takes away the lives of those who get it" (Prov. 1:10-19 NIV).

Lack of judgment with regard to sex: *"I saw among the simple, I noticed among the young men, a youth who lacked judgment. He was going down the street near her corner, walking along in the direction of her house at twilight, as the day was fading, as the dark of night set in. Then out came a woman to meet him, dressed like a prostitute and with crafty intent. (She is loud and defiant, her feet never stay at home; now in the street, now in the squares, at every corner she lurks.) She took hold of him and kissed him and with a brazen face she said: 'I have fellowship offerings* [traditionally, peace offerings] *at home; today I fulfilled my vows. So I came out to meet you; I looked for you and have found you! I have covered my bed with colored linens from Egypt. I have perfumed my bed with myrrh, aloes and cinnamon. Come, let's drink deep of love till morning; let's enjoy ourselves with love! My husband is not at home; he has gone on a long journey. He took his purse filled with money and will not be home till full moon.' With persuasive words she led him astray; she seduced him with her smooth talk. All at once he followed her like an ox going to the slaughter, like a deer* [Syriac (see also Septuagint); Hebrew: fool] *stepping into a noose* [The meaning of the Hebrew for this line is uncertain.] *till an arrow pierces his liver, like a bird darting into a snare, little knowing it will cost him his life. Now then, my sons, listen to me; pay attention to what I say. Do not let your heart turn to her ways or stray into her paths. Many are the victims she has brought down; her slain are a mighty throng. Her house is a highway to the grave,* [Hebrew: Sheol] *leading down to the chambers of death"* (Prov. 7:7-27 NIV).

A key to righteous living: *"How can a young man keep his way pure? By living according to your word"* (Ps. 119:9 NIV).

⋙═◦◉◦═⋘

Mommy's crying,
Daddy's gone.

Mommy is no longer singing a song.
I hurt so bad inside
With you not by my side.
Mommy and Daddy,
Please hear my cry.

Love the children;
Give us a chance.
We are tomorrow;
We deserve a chance.

(Written by Ms. Debbie Bartlett. Used with permission.)

Key Note:

_____

_____

_____

_____

Chapter 15

STORIES OF HOPE

BY DAVID BURROWS

Olympic Moment

I will never forget a scene that unfolded during the Olympics some years ago that demonstrated a parent's love for a grown son who needed help and encouragement. A young man from England (Derek) had trained for years to make it to the Olympics. He made the final in the 400 meters and stood a good chance of getting a medal. With these high hopes, he took off with all the other runners when the gun sounded. As they rounded the turn, however, something in Derek's leg popped and he could no longer continue.

Obviously disappointed and heartbroken, he began to cry and fell onto the track. Then he slowly got up and began to limp around the track. As he cried and limped, a man appeared from out of the stands and ran onto the track, put his arms around Derek, and began to run with him. The race officials tried to escort the man off the track, but he angrily pushed them away

Key Note:

_____

_____

_____

_____

and shouted, "That's my son!" The father then proceeded to complete the race with his son.

It had been a long time since I had cried, but that day I did. It did not matter to that father that his son did not get a medal. He was proud of his son and would not let anything stop him from being there with his son during that difficult and disappointing moment. I am sure it would have been easy for the father to sit in the stands and simply feel sorry for his son. I am not even sure what type of relationship they might have had before this took place. One thing I do know, however, is that the attitude displayed by this man showed how parents should always "be there" for their children in defeat and disappointment as well as in triumph.

That is an Olympic moment I will never forget.

The Funeral

I attended a funeral some years ago and listened as the daughters of a very special friend of mine talked about their dad who had passed away. Instead of hearing about his business and professional exploits or his being a role model in the community, one of the daughters focused on the fact that her daddy played with her in the pool when she was a young girl. Immediately it struck me. The things we believe are important as a parent are often important to us, but not necessarily to our children. They may not remember or even care about what other people view as important. There are some simple things that leave an indelible impression on them and one of them is taking time to do things with them that they care about. The loudest statement you can make as a parent is doing something your children consider important—no matter how trivial it may seem to you.

Father-Son Relationships

When I was very young, my father and I had a very good relationship, but as time went on, our relationship diminished to no relationship at all. The reason we had a good relationship initially was because every day I would be at his food store, working or just hanging around. At other times he would pick me up from school and take us flying. I truly felt special in those days.

We used to be a part of his team at special flying competitions, which were sort of like the "flying Olympics". Each plane engaged in various competitions, including releasing a balloon into the air, then flying after it until the propeller of the plane popped the balloon. We also used a bag of flour to drop "bombs" at a target and spot the landing site where the plane would touch down.

When I became a teenager, I went nowhere with my father. We had very few conversations and most of those conversations were related to times when I got into trouble. Even then, the conversations were not two-way exchanges. I just listened as he warned or threatened me about my behavior. After a while the situation between us really got ugly, and I was thrown out of my house for attempting to assault my father with a beer bottle!

When I became a parent, I determined that I would not let my relationship with my son deteriorate the way it did with my father. So from a very early age my son was always with me. I played a number of sports and whether it was softball or basketball or anything else, he was on the sidelines, threatening the other team, running onto the field to assist his dad or just being a general nuisance.

Key Note:

_____

_____

_____

_____

That was fine with me; he was my nuisance with a purpose. It was a challenge because he never stopped talking or giving instructions, but I was cultivating a relationship that ensured his future teen years would be different from mine.

When I was building our house, I took my son with me, and he would never keep still. He wanted to work. On one of those days, after repeated warnings, he picked up a hammer to help and banged himself in the head! He cut himself so badly that the wound bled profusely. I wiped off the blood, took him to the sea, washed his head, and we had another good talk about following daddy's instructions. Of course he only listened for a few moments, then tried to resume his "duties".

Those times we spent together produced a relationship that was pretty open and unusual for a teen and his father. My son would often ask me how he could help me, if I was preparing for a church service or youth meeting, I never had to ask him if he wanted to go or if he wanted to help. He would always volunteer. When I started my computer company, he was fixing computers better than others twice his age. In fact, by the time he was 14 years old he was as good as some of my technicians. As the years went by, we would often have man-to-man talks.

Father-Daughter Relationships

I did the same with my daughter. She too would be with me almost everywhere I went. They say mothers are smitten by sons and fathers are smitten by daughters. In my case this maxim proved true. Having a daughter was a wonderful experience; my daughter learned early that she was special to her daddy, and she "worked" this fact for all it was worth. I tried everything I could to be firm but fair with her, but somehow "daddy's girl" would soften my heart so she would end up not being disciplined as harshly as my son would be.

Nevertheless, I learned to keep my focus on doing what was right and disciplining her even though she had my heart. She still had to do the dishes and go through the discipline, no matter how much she smiled and said, "Please!" One of the memories that is most precious to both of us is when I took her on a trip with me—just the two of us. We started out going to Miami and renting a nice "souped-up" car and doing a little speeding (not too much) around the city. I also took her to a restaurant where she enjoyed a nice meal, and we had a great conversation with each other.

On that same trip we traveled to St. Louis where we were delayed at the airport for a few hours, so we went to the Admiral's Club and enjoyed some non-alcoholic drinks at the bar, relaxed, and watched TV until our flight was ready. Although we had traveled many times together on family vacations, this trip was special to just the two of us. She remembered it for years and always asked when she could travel with me again.

Another very memorable experience for us was a trip we took just so she could see snow for the first time. Because we're from the Bahamas, where kids never get to see snow, we decided to take a trip to see my son in New York during a period when we knew it would be snowing. It surely did snow, so my daughter saw snow from the moment we touched down in Newark, New Jersey. From Newark we went to Cortland, New York, where we spent the day skiing.

Because my wife had a back problem, it was just my daughter, Davrielle and I, who took ski lessons and spent the day going

Key Note:

_____

_____

_____

_____

up and down the slopes. This may sound simple, but it was one of those special experiences that a teen never forgets. My wife and I took time out of our busy schedule just so she could see the snow and experience skiing. It was not only special for her, but also for us. We had a wonderful time as a family, driving through the mountains, seeing the snow everywhere, and just having fun. Families need to have fun, too. Teens and parents need to do things that are fun for all.

Change Is Possible

I once had a counseling session with the parents of a teenager that was initially very difficult but turned out to be very rewarding. The parents of a young man brought him to me because he was displaying deviant behavior and hanging out with a crowd whose behaviors were questionable. His parents were threatening to put him out of the house and eventually they did so for a short period.

I spent some time counseling with them and gave them advice that was based on my personal experience and professional knowledge as a counselor. I related details from my past to the young man, and told him about the challenges I faced while I was growing up. I told him how I ended up with the wrong crowd, did drugs, and even became a drug dealer.

I shared with him my experience of being thrown out of my house at the age of 15, and gave him advice as to what he could do to change his life. He was initially surprised by my candidness about my own experiences, but he listened intently. I did not know if what I was saying was having an impact at all, but I did my best and recommended to the parents that they give him one more chance, provided he would live up to what I had outlined to him.

About a year later I was at a particular function and I saw his parents. They proceeded to thank me profusely and stated that their son had gone off to school (I believe it was a military school) and had made a complete turnaround in his life.

As they shared their experience, I realized that you never know what the outcome will be. Sometimes you may think a child will never change, but often, even when it seems like they are not listening, the message is getting through.

People thought I would never change. Many of the pastors and counselors who spoke to me probably thought they were not getting through to me at all. The truth is, you may never know what is going on in a teenager's heart or mind. *That is why it is so important to keep trying and never to give up.* Teenagers do hear their parents even if they seem to block them out or ignore them for a time, due to peer pressure and rebellion.

But the power of a mother's prayers and a father's instructions should never be forgotten.

Key Note:

_____

_____

_____

_____

PART IV

Study Guide

STUDY GUIDE OVERVIEW

This Study Guide takes the principles that Myles Munroe has outlined, and the heart of what David Burrows has shared, and merges them into your daily experience.

The first section is a series of questions for you to consider and they are based on Part I, the first five chapters by Myles Munroe. The second section, is a Parent Scrapbook (and Teen Scrapbook) that coincides with what David Burrows has shared in Parts II and III.

The Scrapbook contains:

1. *Inventory Keepsakes* to help you ascertain what you know and what you don't know about your parenting skills and your relationship with your children.

2. *Application Snapshots* to help you discover goals and real-life ways to solve any problems you may be having.

3. *Tracking Trophies*—a tool to record your progress along the journey ahead.

The Scrapbook can also be used with teens. The questions provide your young person an opportunity to evaluate their experiences within your family. Teens can use the same questions but alter them slightly to fit their unique experience.

Unless you are communicating with your teen successfully in intimate areas, the scrapbooks are designed to be individual self-studies—not necessarily to be shared between youth and adult. The meditative and reflective nature of the Scrapbook provides more opportunities for communication on a deeper level.

STUDY QUESTIONS

Chapter 1 – Three Foundational Goals of Parenting

1. The Three Functional Goals of Parenting are: _____
   _____. Explain each of the goals
   in your own words so that your child(ren) are able to understand. _____
   _____
   _____

2. How have your parenting goals aligned with those you listed
   in the previous question? _____
   Where have you succeeded? _____
   _____
   _____

   Where have you failed? _____
   _____
   _____

   Where are you gaining ground? _____
   _____
   _____

3. Do you see your image reflected in your child(ren)? _____
   In what ways? _____
   _____
   _____

   Think of physical, emotional, intellectual, character and
   personality, gifts and talents, and spiritual traits. What traits

give you positive feedback? _____

Which ones would you like to erase? _____

4. Do you see the image of God reflected in your child(ren)? _____ Be specific as to exactly what you see. Which characteristics of the image of God are in both you and your children? _____
Did you help foster any of these characteristics or did they seem to just appear? _____

5. Do you face any fears in your role as a parent? _____
If so, what are they? _____

_____

Think through fears that might be considered small concerns as well as those that might have greater impact on your child's life. Do you feel equipped to handle the areas of concern? _____ Why or why not? _____

_____

6. Do you think it is possible to only do what you see the Father doing in terms of parenting? _____ If Jesus wants us to follow His example and do only the Father's will, how can we align ourselves with our Father in Heaven? _____

_____

What sort of relationship does it take? _____

_____

7. Where do you need God's love to be your antidote to fear? Let's break this down some more. Are there areas where you have trouble letting God love you? _____

_____

Are these the same areas that fear sneaks in to counter your peace? _____ How can you allow God to penetrate your fears with His love? _____

_____

What kind of difference will this make for you personally?

_____

_____

8. What difference would it make in your life if you could live without fear? Think of the scariest places, situations, people, or achievements that could be conquered with the absence of fear. Name these and think about how you can develop the love of God and apply it to your fears. _____

_____

9. What difference do you think it would make in your children's lives if they could live without fear? _____

_____

How can you teach them to remain safe and yet not have fear? _____

_____

What is the difference? _____

_____

10. How well does your "walk" match your "talk"? Are there any areas in which your child would think you are a hypocrite?

_____

How can you correct this? _____
Do you think you might share where you have been wrong and how you hope to change with your child (age dependent, of course)? _____

_____

11. How well do you model love? _____
Does your child know you love him or her so that they would say so very quickly if asked? _____ What are the characteristics of a love relationship between a parent and a child?

_____

What are the characteristics of a love relationship between a person and their God? _____
How are these two relationships similar? _____

How does parental love help us learn about God's love?
_____

12. In what specific ways are you intentional about your parenting? _____
_____

Do you have certain goals or traits that you have trained your child to be or do? _____
_____

Think through goals for every aspect of your parental role. Consider the goals you would set for your child so they will love God and be a contributing member of society. What path can you set so your parenting will be intentional to reach these goals? _____
_____

13. What kind of parenting job did your parents do for you?
_____

In what ways did they model God's love? _____
How did they fail or seem to fail? _____
How have they influenced your parenting positively?
_____

Are there negative influences you would like to get rid of?
_____

14. In what ways have you exposed your sinful nature to your children? _____
_____

How have you influenced them negatively? _____
_____

In what ways can you atone for these negatives? _____
_____

What does God require of you so that you can "come clean"?
_____
_____

If your children have seen and imitated your negative

habits, what can you do to help them know you have repented and want them to repent as well? _____
_____

15. To what extent do you currently parent your child? _____
_____

What percentage of their parenting comes through teachers? _____ Media? _____ Church leaders? _____ Babysitters or daycare workers? _____ Peers? _____ How do these other influences impact your children positively and negatively?
_____

How can you up the percentage of your parenting? As you consider this, be realistic with your commitments and time, but also remain true to the priority of parenting.
_____

16. Think through your marital status. If you are married and living with your spouse, does your child see a picture of Christ and the Church through your marriage? _____
If you are separated or divorced, does your child understand why God created marriage in the first place? Think through discussions you might have to be sure your child understands God's design for marriage and the family.
_____

17. What should be your ultimate goal in raising your child(ren)? _____
_____

What steps have you taken to achieve this goal? _____
_____

What steps do you need to take? Be specific and find someone who will hold you accountable to your goals.
_____
_____

Chapter 2 – Train Up a Child

1. Did you have a plan for training your child to use the potty or to learn their letters or colors? _____
   When you created a plan, were you deliberate and purposeful about the planning? _____ Did you find resources to help you? _____ Did you take the time necessary to bring your child along at the pace they were able to handle comfortably? _____
   How does this same style of training apply to skills that teens need? _____
   How does it differ? _____

2. Where have you received the most information about how to parent? _____
   _____
   God's Word? _____ Your parents? _____ Books? _____ Do you feel your information is adequate? _____
   Is your information distorted in any way? _____
   What information do you need the most to handle situations you face currently? _____
   _____

3. How can you tell the difference between parenting advice that is based on philosophies of men rather than the mind of God? _____
   What distinctive marks do these world views have? _____
   _____
   What are some of the tenets that the Word of God says about parenting that you already know? _____
   _____
   How well are you following what you know? _____
   _____

4. What has been your interpretation of the "Parent's Mandate" in Proverbs 22:6 "*Train a child in the way he shoula*

go, and when he is old he will not turn from it." _____

_____

Is this a promise? _____ A probability? _____ What types of training are inherent in this proverb? _____

_____

What does *"when he is old he will not turn from it"* mean to you?

_____

Does this mean children will never stray or sow their wild oats? _____

5. What are some of the challenges parents face as they try to show the way of righteousness to their children? _____

_____

What challenges have you faced? _____

Why can it be difficult to keep righteousness before your children? _____

_____

Why does it seem as if children desire everything BUT righteousness at times? _____

_____

6. What prerequisite is necessary to show our children the way they should go? _____

_____

Are we ever really "qualified" to show children the way of righteousness? _____

How can we model something that we are still growing in ourselves? _____

_____

Why can it be difficult for you to show your mistakes to your children? _____

_____

Is it embarrassing to let them see you grow? _____

Do you feel obligated to be "mature" in all things and not err in front of your children? _____

7. What legacy do you think you are leaving your children?
_____
What legacy does the Lord expect you to leave them?
_____
If we train our children in the way of the Lord and teach
them to love God with all their hearts, how will this help
them discover their meaning and purpose in life? _____
_____
How will it help them experience citizenship in the
Kingdom of Heaven? _____
_____

8. Why do you think many parents say they believe that the
love of God, love of family, and love of life is what matters
most, yet they spend most of their time striving for material
things? _____
Why must this change? _____
How much time do you spend in either of these directions?
_____
Do you feel you are well-balanced in your priorities?
_____ Do you see any changes that you should make?
_____ If so, what are they? _____

9. Think back to your first seven years of life. What do you
think was instilled in you during this period that has helped
shape your character and worldview today? _____
_____
Are there problem areas that need deliverance or healing?
_____
Are there positive areas that help strengthen your parenting
role?_____

10. What does it mean for children and adults to have "ageless
spirits." _____
_____
How does this concept encourage us to train little children

in the things of God and not wait until they are older? _____

Even though a child's mind is immature, how can they still absorb the spiritual things that we present to them? _____

Has this principle been proven true in your own experience? If so, in what way? _____

11. Evaluate your purpose for being a parent. How well do you love your children? How are you at nurturing them? Are you one who adequately cares for them? How competent are you at training your children to become mature, happy, successful, productive, and well-adjusted adults? _____

12. What is the difference between teaching children responsibility and placing burdens on them they were never meant to carry? _____
Why is "play" important for a child? _____
Think back to your childhood. How well were you taught responsibility? _____

Did you carry any undue burdens? _____
How much were you encouraged to play? _____

13. What are the possible results of thinking that children are merely "pint-sized adults?" _____
How does this affect the child's sense of safety and security? _____

Have you ever been guilty of demanding adult maturity from your children? _____ How can you avoid this improper expectation? _____

14. Contrast the two environments below. First, evaluate what kind of environment you had as you grew up. Secondly, evaluate what kind of environment you are producing in your home today.

ENVIRONMENT 1	ENVIRONMENT 2
No boundaries	Boundaries
Parents who cheat	Parents who have consistent discipline
Parents who are dishonest	Parents who are fair
Parents who belittle	Parents who affirm love
Parents who demean their children	Parents who give challenging, realistic expectations

_____

_____

_____

15. How does someone provoke a child to wrath? _____

_____

What would be the signs that the child is wrathful? _____

_____

How does a parent exasperate or provoke their children if they demonstrate double standards in front of them? _____

_____

How do we provoke our children to wrath when we make unrealistic threats or fail to follow threw with our word?

_____

How does inconsistent discipline hurt children? _____

_____

Have you ever provoked your child to wrath? _____ Have you asked forgiveness for such an act? _____

16. Did your parents ever show favoritism toward one sibling over another? _____ Do you have a favorite child? _____ What are the probable outcomes to the ones who are not favored? _____

To the ones who are favored? _____

Do any of your extended family favor one child over another? _____

How can you address this issue with someone so your children will not have long term effects from this treatment?

_____

Chapter 3 – Principles of Training Children

1. Have you seen multigenerational consequences in your family as a result of how successfully or unsuccessfully parents have raised their children? _____ Have you noticed this long-term impact in other families? _____ Why do you think most parents are shortsighted and think they are impacting only their children and not their children's children? _____

   How would a long-term "family tree" concept of parenting change the way most people would raise their children?

   _____

   How should it change your style of parenting? _____

   _____

2. Child rearing does not only benefit the child, it also benefits parents. How has raising your children benefited you?

   _____

   Name specific ways in which you have had your character developed through parenting. _____

3. Why do you think God has connected the promise of long life to the honor of one's parents? _____

   _____

   Why is honor so important? _____

   Does a child who consistently does wrong honor a parent? _____ How well have you honored your parents?

   _____

4. How were you taught obedience as a child? _____
    Do you use the same method on your children? _____ How
    do you set limits? _____
    How do you teach the value of delayed gratification? _____
    _____
    How do you train your children to think of the needs of others and not just gratify their own desires? _____
    _____

5. How does the process of submission to a parent help children submit to other authorities? _____
    _____
    How well do you submit to authorities, especially when you disagree with them? _____
    How does your submission show others how to submit to God? _____
    How submissive are you to God? _____
    Do your children see this modeled effectively in your life? _____

6. How well did your parents control your behavior? _____
    _____
    Is your household a demonstration of proper control? _____
    _____
    How does proper control maintain respect for you and others? _____
    What control challenge do you face the most in your home?
    _____

7. Do you make control and training appropriate to your children's ages? _____
    How consistent are you in maintaining control? _____
    _____
    Have your children ever seen you disagree with your spouse? _____
    Have they ever played one parent against the other? _____

How much of a buddy are you to your child? _____
What kind of distance do you maintain so that you remain the parent and not the peer? _____
_____

8. How well do you maintain rules of coercion with your children? _____
What is your means of disciplining your children based on their age? _____
What process do you maintain so that you do not punish in anger? _____
How do you avoid breaking your children's spirits when disciplining them? _____
_____
Are you consistent to make the punishment fit the crime?
_____
Are you in control when you mete out the punishment?
_____
Are you careful of the manner in which you physically discipline your children? _____

9. How does discipline provide a future and a hope for your children? _____
_____
How does the love you show them through discipline give them life? _____

10. Rate yourself on the following guidelines for discipline. Score yourself as to whether you follow the guideline: **1** - most of the time, **2** - some of the time, or **3** - hardly at all.
    1. I am consistent _____
    2. I never discipline in anger _____
    3. I treat all my children equally _____
    4. I do not allow my children to despise discipline _____
    5. I do not allow my children to rebel _____   ·

6. I do not allow my children to complain about their discipline _____
7. I do not allow my children to become bitter _____
8. I do not allow my children to become slothful _____
9. I never ask or demand my children to do anything I would not do _____
10. I never ridicule, belittle, scorn, or embarrass my children, especially in public _____

Chapter 4 – Spare Not the Rod

1. As you think back to your childhood, did your parents discipline you constantly or only when necessary? _____
   In the same manner, how do you discipline your children?
   _____
   Do they see love in you when they are disciplined or do they see your anger? _____

2. As a child, were you ever criticized or corrected even when you did nothing wrong? ____ How did that make you feel?
   _____ How does criticizing children when they have done nothing wrong bring insecurity to a child? _____
   _____
   What does a "performance mentality" look like? _____
   Do you see any of this mentality in yourself? _____ In your children? _____

3. How well do you relax with your children? _____
   How easy is it for you to have fun together? _____
   Is it a strain or does fun come easily? _____
   Do you plan "memory making" events and activities with your family? _____ Do they ever refer to activities you have done in the past as something they enjoyed? _____
   _____

4. How often do you give kudos to your child for their accomplishments? _____
How well do you affirm who they are in spite of any problems they have? _____ How many times a week do you tell your children to "wait" when they have things to tell you because you are in the midst of other activities? _____ Do you think your children feel that they are ignored? _____

5. How well do you handle seeing your children make mistakes? _____
Do you tend to overcorrect them? _____ Do you affirm who they are, when you correct them? _____
Do you have trouble not humiliating them when they are wrong? _____ Do they see you admit your own mistakes? _____

6. Do you see your hands as extensions of God's hands? _____ How does this principle determine whether you should hit your child with your hand or not? _____
_____
Do you have a "rod" or implement of punishment that is appropriate and recognized by your children? _____
_____

7. How do you maintain a love focus when disciplining a child?
_____
How do you control anger when you mete out discipline?
_____
What changes in attitude or behavior do you expect when you have disciplined your children? _____
Do you get the results you are looking for? _____ What do you think needs to change about the way in which you discipline your children? _____
_____

8. Do you explain why you are punishing your child when you discipline him or her? _____
    Do you tend to make each time of discipline a counseling session? _____
    What does that tend to produce in a child? _____
    _____

    What are the concrete areas that you can communicate with your child during the time of correction? _____
    _____

    Do your children always know that you are disciplining them for their own good and not in order to hurt them? ____
    _____

9. Are you a parent who lets your children cry when they are receiving discipline? _____
    How can crying benefit your child? _____
    _____

    What does it show about the child's view of the situation?
    _____

    Are you quick to comfort your children when they cry following a punishment? _____

10. How does an undisciplined childhood result in destructive behaviors later on in life? _____
    _____

    What boundaries do you think are profitable for your children to learn when they are young that have direct correlations to what they will need as adults? _____
    _____

11. What is the difference between submission and breaking a child's will? _____
    _____

    How can you encourage submission and avoid breaking the will of your child? _____
    _____

How does correction help children understand right and wrong? _____

How does correction minister to the unity of the body, soul and spirit? _____

How does punishment penetrate to the child's very identity? _____

12. What tendencies do your children have toward foolishness? _____

How can correction drive foolishness out of a child? _____

When children are out of control, what does this usually say about their parents' form of correction? _____ _____

Chapter 5 – In Wisdom, Stature, and Favor

1. Why do you think God chose marriage and parenting to be the means of human procreation and training? _____ _____

As God's chosen vessel to fulfill these purposes, do you take the responsibility with His plan in mind? _____ _____

2. Why do you think God sent Jesus as a baby and not as a man? _____

What purpose did it serve to give Jesus the life of a child? _____

What can we learn from Mary and Joseph's example? _____ _____

3. *"...Mary and Joseph were faithful, regular, and consistent in their worship of God."* Can the same be said about you? _____
Jesus reflected these disciplines in his character at the age

of 12. Do your children reflect these same disciplines? _____ Why or why not? _____

4. Jesus showed proper respect to the elders in the Temple. Do your children respect and honor the leaders at your church? _____ Do your children see you modeling respect and honor toward your pastor? _____ Have you spoken against the pastor or other leaders in front of them? _____

_____

5. Jesus obeyed Mary and Joseph and went home with them. He exercised His freewill to obey. What was the result? _____

_____
How well do your children subject their own desires to yours and obey? _____
Do they exercise their freewill to obey or are they under coercion? _____

6. In which four areas did Jesus grow in as He matured? _____

_____
As you look at your life, how have you grown in these four areas? _____

_____
Are you still growing in them? _____ Do your children see you growing? _____ Is the evidence of your growth plain to see or hidden?_____

7. How much time have you spent instructing your child(ren) how to eat properly? _____
Do they know what is good for them and what is not? _____ How much time have you spent training your child(ren) to eat spiritual food? _____ What has your process been to encourage them to feast on the Word of God? _____
What can you do to increase their desire toward spiritual things? _____

8.   What does it mean that our "spirits are ageless?" _____
_____

How does this truth make it possible for little ones to receive
the Word of God? _____
_____

Does this truth break the traditional way Christian parents
train their children in the Scriptures? _____
_____

9.   Why is imparting wisdom the #1 priority for parents? _____
_____

What does wisdom mean in terms of spiritual things? _____
_____

How does the application of wisdom take place? _____
_____

How is wisdom different from knowing a lot of information
or being intelligent? _____
How do you impart wisdom to your child(ren)? _____
_____

What books of the Bible contain the greatest wealth of wisdom? _____
How often do you read these books? _____ How can we
ensure that Scripture wisdom will be absorbed into the subconscious and spirit of our children? _____
_____

10. What is stature? _____
How does stature relate to physical characteristics and physical development? _____ How
does discipline play into the concept of stature?
_____ Think about the way you grew physi-
cally as a child and a teen. Did your parents instruct you
about body discipline? _____
How well do you teach your children about taking care of
their bodies? _____

11. Define self-control in your own words. _____
_____

    Since we are weak by nature, how can we perfect the discipline of self control? _____
    _____

    How well do you exercise self control over your body, your mind, your emotions, your tongue, your activities? _____
    _____

    Do your children see someone who models self control? ___
    _____

    Do they want to model you in this area? _____
    _____

12. How does self-control play itself out when teens are tempted with drugs, tobacco, alcohol, and sex? _____
    _____

    By teaching self-control and rewarding our children who exercise it, is it possible to establish the patterns in their lives before they are faced with dangerous choices? _____
    _____

    How will this help them? _____
    _____

13. What does self-control have to do with our relationships?
    _____

    How is self control reflected in honesty? _____
    In being fair? _____
    In acts of kindness? _____
    In being generous? _____
    How can we help our children establish the self-control that brings this kind of fruit? _____
    _____

14. It may be hard for us to imagine Jesus being tempted as we are. Understanding His needs can help our children relate to Jesus and the strength that He can provide them. How

would you explain to your teen that Jesus might have wanted to overeat? _____

_____

How would you explain that Jesus had a sex drive? _____

_____

How would you explain to your teen that Jesus took no short cuts to maturity but had to learn through discipline—just as they do? _____

_____

15. How does wisdom relate to stature and its discipline? _____

_____

How do these two work together to produce maturity? _____

_____

If we do not help our children gain wisdom and develop the stature of discipline, what might be the results? _____

_____

What do you need to do to develop these in your child(ren)? _____
How will you give them the practical side to wisdom? _____

_____

How will you help them determine their priorities? _____

_____

How will you train them to know how and when to apply self-discipline in their lives? _____

_____

16. In your own words, explain what *favor with God* is. _____

_____

How do you know if you have favor with God? _____

_____

Have you experienced His favor in concrete ways? _____

_____

Have you shared these incidents of favor with your children?

_____

How can you increase your ability to model how His favor works toward you? _____

_____

17. How well do you trust God? _____ In what areas is it difficult to trust God? _____ _____Where is it easiest to trust Him? _____ How do you develop trust? _____ Does your family know how much you trust God? _____ Are they inspired by your trust? _____ How can you show your children how to develop trust in God in their daily affairs?

_____

18. Do your children see you read the Bible daily? _____ Do they see you pray? _____ Do they understand the value you place on church and the community of faith? _____ Do they sense that God is your first priority? _____ What steps might you take to increase your visibility on these items? _____

19. Think back to when you were your children's ages. Did you have a relationship with God then? _____ If so, what was the relationship like? _____ What characterized your walk with God? _____ _____ Do you feel your children can mature in spiritual things? _____ What resources may help stimulate their interest and desire to press into God? _____ How can you fan the flames of their spirits so they will fall in love with Jesus to a greater degree? _____

_____

20. Do you have favor with other people? _____ Do people seem to like you and want to be around you? _____ Is this just a personality trait or has God given you favor? _____ What is the difference between having favor with people

and being a "man-pleaser"? _____

How can you distinguish the difference? _____

What is the motivation behind pleasing men? _____

_____ What is the motivation behind having favor with others? _____ How can you teach your children the difference? _____

_____

21. If you took an inventory of what your children are currently learning from you, what would it look like? _____

_____

Now go back over your Study Guide answers and tally the negative and the positive influence you are having on your children. But don't be discouraged if you find yourself lacking. God has entrusted you with your children and there is sufficient time to make necessary changes, whether subtle or severe. Think about ways to change the negatives to positives. Remember, work on yourself and let your children see your progress.

22. "There is no substitute for parental influence in the lives of children." Having read this book, what does this concept mean to you now? _____

_____

_____

_____

PART I—PARENT SCRAPBOOK

Scrapbooks usually contain photos, keepsakes, and memories. These collections give us a "bird's eye view" of our lives. The following scrapbook is a tool to accomplish the same purpose. Use it to track what has happened and what is happening in your family. Then use it to record what will happen in the future. The scrapbook is designed for families with teenagers. You could adapt it for younger children by making age-appropriate changes in the questions. You might want to create a three-ring binder of the scrapbook items.

Inventory Keepsakes

This section is designed to record two important things: what you know and what you don't know. By thinking through each part, you will be better equipped to evaluate how effective you are in your role as parent.

A. What I Know.

When you look at mementos from a vacation or activity, you are reminded of what you actually did. Take an honest look at what you see. Don't cover over anything you would like to do better and don't exaggerate things that aren't so bad. Take notes about each area so you can refer to them later.

1. **Characteristics about the teen:**

   How much is your teen's conscience tuned in to God?

   _____

   a. How does your teen behave when you are absent?

   _____

b. In what areas are you able to trust your teen implicitly? In what areas does your trust waver? _____
_____

c. What are your teen's gifts? Talents? Training? _____
_____

d. What are your teen's best character traits? What are the worst traits your teen has? _____
_____

e. How open is your teen to instruction? Is your teen's heart soft and teachable? _____
_____

f. What fruit of the Spirit does your teen exhibit? _____
_____

g. What gifts of the Spirit does your teen portray? _____
_____

h. If you could choose just one thing that you would like to change about your teen, what would it be?
_____

i. What is your teen's favorite: (If you don't know some of these, transfer them down to the next section for research.)
Pastime _____
Sport _____
Food _____
Color _____
Friend _____
Book of the Bible _____
Bible character _____
Hero _____
Family member _____
Book _____
Movie _____
Song _____
Game _____

Vacation or Experience _____

Friend _____

Clothes _____

TV Show _____

Singing group or band (sacred or secular)

_____

2. **Memories of supernatural moments in the teen's life:**

   Take some time to think through the life of your child,
   year by year. Consider any extraordinary times when
   there were supernatural moments in your teen's life.
   This may refer to a miracle or deliverance or protection
   or achievement beyond his or her own ability. Instead of
   just quickly checking these off, savor the memory by
   replaying the scene or situation and remembering how
   you felt and how your teen felt. God's intervention cannot be imitated!

3. **Memories of birth:**

   Allow yourself to go back and remember your teen's
   birth. (If you have adopted the child, remember the first
   moment you saw him or her.) Remind yourself of your
   feelings, your dreams, your hopes for their future, your
   plans for caring for the child and your excitement at the
   possibilities that lay before you. Recapture those feelings
   and look at a current picture of your teen and regain any
   hope that has been lost. Rework the excitement into
   your soul so you are ready for the next adventure.

B. What I Do *Not* Know.

This part will require research. If your teen will not be
offended, ask the questions outright, but make sure it is part
of a discussion and don't disagree with the answers. Let
them freely share how they feel. Whether their perceptions

are right or wrong, it reflects how they feel and that is truth in and of itself. You could also give them a paper with questions on it and ask them to write their answers, which may make them feel freer to answer without trying to fulfill any expectations from you or in order to avoid any reactions from you. You also can research certain information online. Do not talk to your teen's friends unless they give you permission. Transfer anything you did not know from the "Part A" here so you can discover the answers.

1. Research their favorites things.

2. Find out what your teen's priorities are.

3. Discover what goals your teen has for the next month, school year, next summer, two years from now.

4. Research your teen's friends: Who are they and what activity do they do together? What are their families like? Who does your teen confide in?

5. Research what they like least:
   About themselves _____
   About school _____
   About church _____
   About your family _____

6. Research what they think about basic tenets of faith:
   Salvation _____
   God as the only God _____
   Jesus as the only way to God _____
   The Holy Spirit _____
   The Bible's accuracy _____
   The Church's purpose _____
   Heaven and Hell _____
   Kingdom Living _____
   Etc. _____

7. Find out what your children are doing. Ask how they spend most of their leisure hours. If they were totally free from school or work, how would they choose to spend their hours? _____

    _____

8. Get their perspectives on things. Find out what your teen thinks about current event issues. Ask them what they think the biggest issue in America is. What is the biggest issue for the Church today? Find out what they think about their future, and about other members of the family.

From the answers to these questions, you may have to do further research. If you are not familiar with their answers, discover why your teen likes or dislikes certain things. Check out their favorite singing group or band. Find out the lyrics to their favorite song(s). Read descriptions of their favorite movie—or better yet, rent it and watch it. Take the time to put yourself in your teen's shoes and see what you can learn about their identity.

Application Snapshots

This section is an action plan. Like "action shot" photos, you may find these snapshots can be exciting. They can open up a new adventure for you and your teen. This section is divided into two parts. The first part is what you need to do to get to the next level of solving some problems or pressing forward in your parenting skills. The second part is geared toward your active involvement in specific, directed prayer for your parenting skills and your children.

A. What I Need to Do.

Be creative with what you have at your disposal. This can make the adventure more meaningful. This does not need to take a lot of money.

1. Gather resources that your teen might like or has expressed a desire to have. These may be books or movies, articles that answer some of their questions, games, or activities. Enjoy them together as a family.

2. Provide positive experiences based on what they like to do. Some families schedule family nights once a week. Others do more spontaneous events and activities. However you design it, make sure it is realistic and achievable based on your time constraints. And don't try to milk the experience for all it's worth. Give your teen the opportunity to evaluate whether they truly like the experience or activity based on its own merit. Positive experiences can be as simple as a walk in the park or as complicated as planning the next family vacation.

3. Provide safe times with friends. Show your teen that you want them to have friends by opening your home (your car, your food, and your heart) to their friends. Encourage them to invite their friends over and be sure to have favorite snacks on hand. Volunteer to chaperone or drive them to places. Listen to what they laugh about and how they communicate with each other.

4. Provide time—quantity and quality. Schedule your time so you are available to your teen. Most teens want the availability of their parents more than they want a quality planned experience. They want to know that you will watch them play soccer or sit around waiting for their trumpet lesson to be over. This speaks love to them more than gifts. But do plan some quality time as well. Get alone with your teen and have a soda at the favorite

hangout, without other family members vying for your attention.

5. Try to correct things that your teen likes least. Whenever possible eliminate immediately those things that the teen does not like. Certain foods or clothes or expectations that are not important. Things that are non-negotiable should remain and the teen needs to know why.

6. Surprise your teen each week. This may be stilted at first, but it can be a lot of fun. Try taking them to a favorite movie or sports event, or make their favorite dinner. Or let them know you are eliminating something they do not like from their chore roster.

B. What I Need to Pray.

This is perhaps the most important aspect of all to your growth as a parent. Make time to pray for your family members each day. Some suggestions follow.

1. Picture your child's heart like a garden. What things need to be tenderly watered and cultivated? What things need the sun of God's Word and truth? What things need the experience of the rain of time and energy to grow? What things are like weeds that need pulled? What things need pruning in order to establish further growth? Answering these questions will help you establish prayer goals and be open to God's instruction how to accomplish these garden chores for your child's heart in the days to come.

2. Pray about faith issues. Begin with your issues of faith. Ask God to lead you into a greater dimension of trust so

you can believe for the impossible. Then you can pray for your teen's issues of faith.

3. Pray about any friend issues. If you have concerns about your teen's friends, be sure to ask the Lord to give you a heart for those friends and His perspective on their needs. (This is not necessarily the same as what you see in the flesh.) Then allow Him to direct your prayers.

4. Pray about any values issues. Begin with any issues you have in being firm in your own values system. Then pray for your teen's set of values and how you would like to see them change.

5. Pray for your teen's grades and school work. First pray for your diligence to increase in your job, home, and ministry. Then pray that your teen would desire to excel and be the person God has intended.

6. When you pray, use God's Word so that your prayers will totally be in His will. Use at least one of these Scriptures every day of the month and pray for yourself and your family:

Genesis 1:26-28 (NIV). *Then God said, "Let us make man in our image, in our likeness;…So God created man in his own image, in the image of God he created him; male and female he created them. God blessed them and said to them, "Be fruitful and increase in number; fill the earth and subdue it. Rule over the fish of the sea and the birds of the air and over every living creature that moves on the ground."*

Genesis 5:1-3 (NIV). *This is the written account of Adam's line. When God created man, he made him in the likeness of God. He created them male and female and blessed them. And when they were created, he called them "man." When Adam* *had lived 130 years, he had a son in his own likeness, in his own image; and he named him Seth.*

John 14:9 (NIV). *"...Anyone who has seen me has seen the Father...."*

Colossians 1:15 (NIV). *He is the image of the invisible God, the firstborn over all creation.*

1 John 4:16-18 (NIV). *God is love. Whoever lives in love lives in God, and God in him. In this way love is made complete among us so that we will have confidence on the day of judgment, because in this world we are like Him. There is no fear in love. But perfect love drives out fear, because fear has to do with punishment. The one who fears is not made perfect in love.*

Proverbs 20:11 (NIV). *Even a child is known by his actions, by whether his conduct is pure and right.*

Ephesians 5:1-2 (NIV). *Be imitators of God, therefore, as dearly loved children and live a life of love, just as Christ loved us and gave Himself up for us as a fragrant offering and sacrifice to God.*

Proverbs 22:15 (NKJV). *Foolishness is bound up in the heart of a child; The rod of correction will drive it far from him.*

Malachi 2:10,14,15 (NIV). *Have we not all one Father? Did not one God create us? Why do we profane the covenant of our fathers by breaking faith with one another? ...the Lord is acting as the witness between you and the wife of your youth, because you have broken faith with her, though she is your partner, the wife of your marriage covenant. Has not the Lord made them one? In flesh and spirit they are His. And why one? Because He was seeking godly offspring. So guard yourself in your spirit, and do not break faith with the wife of your youth.*

Ephesians 5:31-32 (NIV). *"For this reason a man will leave his father and mother and be united to his wife, and the two will become one flesh." This is a profound mystery—but I am talking about Christ and the church.*

Proverbs 22:6 (NIV). *Train a child in the way he should go, and when he is old he will not turn from it.*

Proverbs 29:15 (NIV). *The rod of correction imparts wisdom, but a child left to himself disgraces his mother.*

Ephesians 6:1-4 (NIV). *Children, obey your parents in the Lord, for this is right. "Honor your father and mother"—which is the first commandment with a promise—"that it may go well with you and that you may enjoy long life on the earth." Fathers, do not exasperate your children; instead, bring them up in the training and instruction of the Lord.*

Proverbs 19:18 (NIV). *Discipline your son, for in that there is hope; do not be a willing party to his death.*

Proverbs 13:24 (NKJV). *He who spares his rod hates his son, But he who loves him disciplines him promptly.*

Proverbs 23:13-14 (NIV). *Do not withhold discipline from a child; if you punish him with the rod, he will not die. Punish him with the rod and save his soul from death.*

Hebrews 12:11 (NIV). *No discipline seems pleasant at the time, but painful. Later on, however, it produces a harvest of righteousness and peace for those who have been trained by it.*

Proverbs 22:15 (NKJV). *Foolishness is bound up in the heart of a child; The rod of correction will drive it far from him.*

Luke 2:52 (NKJV). *And Jesus increased in wisdom and stature, and in favor with God and men.*

John 6:63 (NKJV). *...The words that I speak to you are spirit, and they are life.*

Proverbs 17:6 (NIV). *Children's children are a crown to the aged, and parents are the pride of their children.*

Colossians 3:20 (NIV). *Children, obey your parents in everything, for this pleases the Lord.*

1 Timothy 5:4 (NIV). *But if a widow has children or grandchildren, these should learn first of all to put their religion into practice by caring for their own family and so repaying their parents and grandparents, for this is pleasing to God.*

Deuteronomy 29:29 (NIV). *The secret things belong to the Lord our God, but the things revealed belong to us and to our children forever, that we may follow all the words of this law.*

Joshua 4:6 (NIV). *to serve as a sign among you. In the future, when your children ask you, 'What do these stones mean?'*

Psalm 8:2 (NIV). *From the lips of children and infants you have ordained praise because of your enemies, to silence the foe and the avenger.*

Psalm 34:11 (NIV). *Come, my children, listen to me; I will teach you the fear of the Lord.*

Psalm 78:4 (NIV). *We will not hide them from their children; we will tell the next generation the praiseworthy deeds of the Lord, his power, and the wonders he has done.*

Psalm 103:13 (NIV). *As a father has compassion on his children, so the Lord has compassion on those who fear him;*

Proverbs 20:7 (NIV). *The righteous man leads a blameless life; blessed are his children after him.*

Psalm 25:7 (NIV). *Remember not the sins of my youth and my rebellious ways; according to your love remember me, for you are good, O Lord.*

Read Psalms, Proverbs, and Ecclesiastes frequently. To start on this path, the following reading schedule for the next 31 days is offered.

Day	Psalms	Proverbs	Ecclesiastes
1	1-5	1	1:1-11
2	2-10	2	1:12-18
3	11-15	3	2:1-11
4	16-20	4	2:12-17
5	21-25	5	2:18-26
6	26-30	6	3:1-11
7	31-35	7	3:12-22
8	36-40	8	4:1-6
9	41-45	9	4:7-16
10	46-50	10	5:1-9
11	51-55	11	5:10-18
12	56-60	12	6:1-6
13	61-65	13	6:7-12
14	66-70	14	7:1-14
15	71-75	15	7:15-18
16	76-80	16	7:19-22
17	81-85	17	7:23-29
18	86-90	18	8:1-9
19	91-95	19	8:10-13
20	96-100	20	8:14-17
21	101-105	21	9:1-6
22	106-110	22	119:7-12
23	111-115	23	9:13-18
24	116-118	24	10:1-7
25	119	25	10:8-15
26	120-125	26	10:16-20
27	126-130	27	11:1-5
28	131-135	28	11:6-8
29	136-140	29	11:9-10
30	141-145	30	12:1-8
31	146-150	31	12:9-14

Remember, you can only change what you think and do, not what your teen thinks and does. This means that you must lead by example. Read the verses in the Scriptures about parenting and leave the verses about being a youth to your teen's reading time. If you set your face like flint toward fulfilling the verses outlined for parents, many of your teen's issues will come to rest.

Track Trophies

This section gives you a means to track answers to prayer, victories along your journey, and requests that you have made to God. Be sure to date your entries so you can quantify the way God has worked on your behalf and how you have been obedient to God's plan for you as a parent—and point you toward a future.

A. What God Has Done! Get your trophy!

1. Record answers to prayer—no victory is too small.

   _____

   _____

   _____

   _____

2. Record application activities, events or resources you procured and your teen's reactions.

   _____

   _____

   _____

   _____

3. Record changes in your teen.

   _____

   _____

_____

_____

B. What God Will Do!

1. Record prayer requests.

   _____

   _____

   _____

   _____

2. Record any "to dos" you are intentionally planning.

   _____

   _____

   _____

   _____

3. Jot down any creative ideas about what God will do in your life and the life of your teen.

   _____

   _____

   _____

   _____

PART II—TEEN SCRAPBOOK

Go through each topic of the Parent Scrapbook and discover some things about your parent that you may not know. You may have to adapt the questions slightly—like find out what their favorite band was when they were in high school (not currently), etc. When you get to the Application Snapshots, plan to surprise your parent each week. You could write a short note or an e-mail, or you could meet one of their goals each week. When you get to the Track Trophies section, be sure to read the verses of Scripture pertaining to youth.

Journaling and Notes